DATE DUE

10	30	01	
2/13/06			

Egypt

Editor Lesley Firth
Design Patrick Frean
Picture Research Maggie Colbeck
                 Lorna Collin
Production Philip Hughes
            Vivienne Driscoll
Illustrations Ron Hayward Associates
            Allard Design Group
            Patrick Frean
            Sally Launder
            Peter Mousdale
            Tony Payne
            Laura Potter
            John Shackell
Maps Matthews and Taylor Associates
Consultants Peter Field
             Fawzi Shafei

The endpaper shows the smaller rock temple at Abu Simbel, with colossi of Ramses II and his queen, Nefertari.

The photograph opposite the list of contents shows a street scene in colourful Old Cairo.

Photographic sources Key to positions of illustrations: *(T)* top, *(C)* centre, *(B)* bottom, *(L)* left, *(R)* right.
J. Allan Cash *21 (BR)*, *27(TR)*. Camera Press *50(T)*, *53(B)*. Colour Library International *2-3*, *36-7(T)*. Egypt Air *43(BR)*. Egyptian Tourist Office *22(T)*, *48(T)*. Mary Evans Picture Library *38(L)*, *39(BR)*. Robert Harding Associates *43(TR)*, *49(BR)*. Alan Hutchison *10-11(B)*, *16(BL)*, *20(BL)*, *21(TL)*, *40(BR)*. A.F. Kersting *16(BR)*. Keystone *43(BL)*, *46(BC)*, *46-7(B)*, *47(T)*, *47(BR)*, *51(TR)*, *52(BL)*. Kobal Collection *40(BL)*. Tom Lonsdale *8(BL)*, *9(TR)*, *9(TL)*, *11(BR)*, *12(BR)*, *13(TL)*, *13(TR)*, *13(BR)*, *15(TL)*, *15(TR)*, *15(BR)*, *15(BL)*, *17(BL)*, *17(TR)*, *18-19(T)*, *22(B)*, *23(TR)*, *23(BR)*, *24(B)*, *25(TR)*, *25(B)*, *26(B)*, *26-7(T)*, *27(BL)*, *27(TC)*, *27(BR)*, *28(TL)*, *28(BL)*, *28(BR)*, *29(TL)*, *30(CR)*, *30(BL)*, *31(TR)*, *32(T)*, *33(L)*, *33(BR)*, *40(TR)*, *42(BL)*, *44(BL)*, *45(TR)*, *45(BL)*, *49(TL)*, *49(TR)*, *49(BL)*, *52(CR)*. William MacQuitty *9(BR)*, *14(BR)*, *17(TL)*, *34(TL)*, *34(BR)*, *35(BL)*, *42(BR)*, *44(T)*, *45(TL)*, *52-3(T)*. Mansell Collection *36-7(B)*, *37(TC)*, *38(BR)*, *39(TL)*, *41(R)*. Middle East Archive *42-3(T)*. Dennis Moore *11(TL)*, *14(TL)*, *29(BL)*, *31(TL)*, *53(TR)*. ZEFA *6-7*, *14(TR)*, *19(BL)*, *19(BR)*, *21(TR)*, *29(TR)*, *45(BR)*. Popperfoto *46(BL)*. Radio Times Hulton Picture Library *37(TR)*, *39(BL)*, *39(TR)*, *41(BL)*, *46(TL)*, *51(TL)*. Ronan Picture Library *8(TL)*. Servizio Editoriale Fotografico *25(TL)*, *33(TR)*. Sarah Tyzack *35(BR)*, *50(BL)*. United Nations *18(BR)*, *48(B)*. Verity Weston *37(BR)*. Terry Williams *23(BL)*, *26(TL)*.

First published 1975
Macdonald Educational Limited
Holywell House
London, E. C. 2

© Macdonald Educational
Limited 1975

ISBN 0 356 05106 4

Published in the United States by Silver Burdett Company, Morristown, N. J.
1977 Printing

Library of Congress
Catalog Card No. 77-70186

Egypt

the land and its people

Michael von Haag

Macdonald Educational

Contents

Egypt, gift of the river

The ribbon of life

In size, Egypt is larger than any European country except Russia. However, fourteen-fifteenths of its area is dry and barren desert where only a few oasis-dwellers and nomadic bedouin can survive. Effectively, Egypt is no wider than the valley of the Nile and its delta. Along this slender ribbon of cultivable land lives 95 per cent of the population.

The ancient Egyptians described their country as having the shape of a lotus plant. The river was like the stem, the Faiyum Oasis was like the bud, and the delta was like the flower.

From time immemorial the Nile overflowed its banks each summer, depositing rich layers of mud upon the fields where the *fellahin* (peasants) ceaselessly irrigated their crops. The river enabled the fields to yield as many as five harvests a year.

Controlling the Nile

In 1966 the Nile overflowed for the last time. The High Dam at Aswan now regulates its flow. With water in reserve, Egypt hopes to increase its cultivable land by one-third and prime its new industries with hydro-electric power. In place of the annual deposit of fertile mud, chemical fertilizer is being manufactured from air and limestone from the desert.

Egypt's future, like its past and its present, will be determined by human ingenuity in finding new applications for the river, nature's gift.

▲ The High Dam now controls the flow of the Nile. In the past, nilometers measured the rising level. A high Nile meant a good harvest, a low Nile could mean starvation.

▼ Egypt is a rainless country, a desert land which is green only along the fringes of the river. So intensive are the irrigation efforts of the fellahin that at some times of the year not a single drop of Nile water escapes into the Mediterranean.

Agriculture in the Delta

Bedouin in the desert

▲ The Nile is the longest river in the world. It flows over 4,000 miles (6,437 km) from Lake Victoria to the Mediterranean. Its tributary, the Blue Nile, swells with the torrential summer rains of Ethiopia and dams up the placid waters of the White Nile at Khartoum. As the Blue Nile ebbs, the White Nile's waters are released, so that Egypt receives an extended flow throughout the summer.

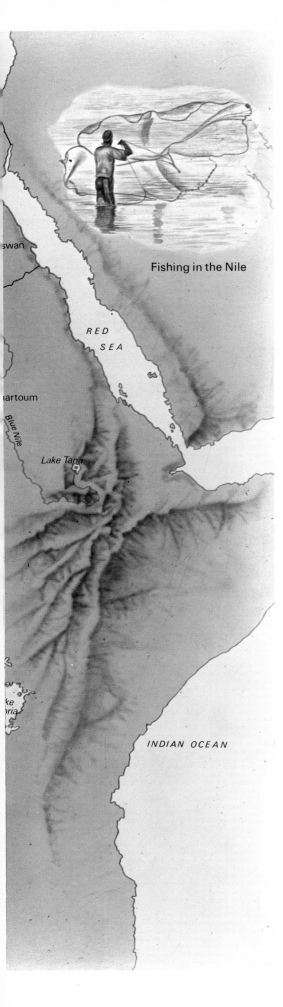

► The Nile is a major transport artery. *Feluccas* like this one have plied the river for thousands of years, downstream on the current, upstream with the winds.

▼ Now, as in pharaonic times, a fellah uses a *shaduf* for lifting water from the river to irrigate his fields. Mechanical pumps are beyond the means of most fellahin.

Fishing in the Nile

▼ After America refused aid, the High Dam at Aswan was built with Russian assistance. It is one of the largest dams in the world. It was constructed out of 17 times as much material as the Great Pyramid.

The dawn of history

▼ The kings of Upper Egypt wore the white crown, while the kings of Lower Egypt wore the red crown. After the conquest of the Delta by Menes, pharaohs wore the Double Crown with the ureaus, or guardian cobra, on the front to symbolize unification.

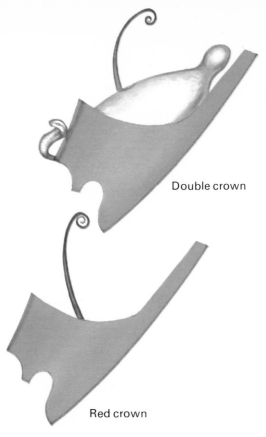

Double crown

White crown

Red crown

Climatic change

About ten thousand years ago, a dramatic change in climate caused the once-fertile lands of northern Africa and the Middle East to turn to dust. Rock drawings found in the Sahara show ancient people hunting deer where now there is only sand. The inhabitants of this land migrated towards the few remaining rivers as the land turned to desert. From the west, across Africa, and from the north, down from the Levant, came the earliest settlers of the Nile Valley and the Delta.

The Nile settlers

The early Egyptians lived a life of prosperity and security on the fertile banks of the Nile. They were protected from foreign menace by the deserts to the east, west and south, and by the Mediterranean to the north, a forbiddingly vast sea for the ancients.

By the third millennium B.C., the Egyptians had developed an elaborate agricultural system based on canals, irrigation channels and the anticipation of the annual renewal of the fields by the river's mud.

Creation of the nation state

The country remained an assortment of feuding tribes and villages, loosely organized into the kingdoms of Upper Egypt (the Valley) and Lower Egypt (the Delta). Around 3000 B.C., an Upper Egyptian King called Menes conquered the Delta, and founded the new capital of Memphis (near modern Cairo). He created a sense of national unity which has persisted in Egypt to the present day.

Secure, prosperous, and ruled by a strong central authority, Egypt was able to undertake great engineering works. The belief in immortality, if only the physical remains of the dead could be preserved, led to the construction of elaborate tombs and the pyramids, the wonders of the ancient world.

▲ This palette shows Menes with his arm upraised to strike the enemy. To the right, an early hieroglyph explains that the falcon god Horus (Menes) has captured (rope around man's neck) the people of the Delta (papyrus symbols).

▼ The year-round sunshine and warm climate, the rich alluvial soil along the Nile, and the intensive labours of the fellahin, have combined to produce abundant harvests like this one illustrated in a pharaonic fresco.

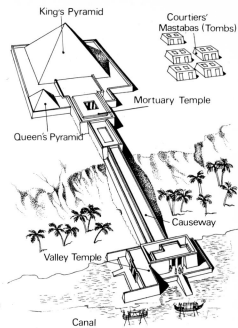

▲ The pyramid, containing the burial chamber of the pharaoh, was only one part of a large funerary complex. The body of the pharaoh was taken by river to the mortuary temple and mummified before burial.

▲ Pyramid construction involved sophisticated engineering knowledge and backbreaking labour. The Great Pyramid of Cheops took 20 years to build. Shifts of one-hundred thousand men were employed at a time.

▲ The Sphinx at Giza was hewn from a natural outcrop of limestone during the IVth Dynasty (c.2620 B.C.). It bears the head either of the pharaoh Chephren or of a god. The combination of human head and lion's body represents wisdom and strength.

The Sphinx is the largest statue surviving from ancient times. Its length is 190 ft (58 m) and its height is 66 ft (20 m). For centuries it lay half-buried in the sand. Though suffering from weather and man, it continues to watch over the Giza necropolis.

The Egyptian character

▶ Bargaining determines not only the price, but the worth of the buyer and the seller. An offer of too much can be more offensive than an offer of too little. It shows the buyer is a fool, and destroys mutual esteem.

▼ Egyptians enjoy being hospitable to one another. The close and friendly ways of the countryside are evident even in city life.

▲ Egyptians are not aggressive, but *baksheesh* is expected for services rendered. Sometimes tourists pay *baksheesh* simply to be left alone.

▶ Egyptian men take pleasure in sitting at a cafe, drinking coffee and smoking strong tobacco in a *nargile*, or water-pipe.

Friendly and easy-going

Most Egyptians live, or have lived, in close-knit rural communities where hostility, envy, or even distance between people could prove disruptive to social life. So Egyptians try hard to be well thought of and to be regarded as generous and friendly, which most of them genuinely are.

The Egyptians are not an aggressive people. If a fight should break out, a crowd gathers and the tumult is allowed to grow. Before further trouble develops, a bystander inevitably calls out "Istafurla" ("Peace for God's sake!") and the combatants are at once reconciled. The year-round heat discourages over-exertion. The Arabic word *bukra* is like the Spanish word *mañana*. It expresses the notion that it is better to take it easy and, if possible, to do tomorrow what could be done today.

Great determination

The Egyptians are tenacious. The fellahin work long, hard days throughout the year, making the land bear fruit. Egyptians are ambitious, both for themselves and for their country. They are great believers in education. It is used against outmoded traditions and to assimilate Western achievements. Egyptians are tolerant of the great diversity of backgrounds in their population, and put patriotism before religion or race. Egyptians are proud of their country, and in view of the problems they continue to overcome, their pride is justified.

▼ This policeman wisely chooses to keep calm. Rush hour pedestrians ignore the traffic lights, and all he can do is to save oncoming cars from being trampled underfoot!

▲ The Egyptian fellahin, living close to the land and reliant on animal-power, have great concern for their animals. It is not unusual to find both family and animals sleeping together under one roof.

▼ Urban life is never distant from the desert. Sandstorms frequently cover streets and rooftops with layers of dust. With no rain to wash it away, it lingers and makes breathing unpleasant. In Cairo and Alexandria, water trucks damp down the dust with their spray.

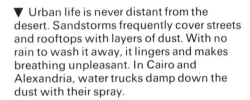

▲ A) The Nubians are an agricultural people of Upper Egypt, though many now work in city hotels and restaurants.

B) The Bedouin are descended from Arab tribes and still prefer the nomadic desert life.

C) Other Arabs are town-dwellers by tradition and engage in trade and commerce.

A religious nation

◀ Cairo's Mohammed Ali Mosque with its dome and slender minarets was designed in the last century by a Greek in the Turkish style. In the foreground is the Sultan Hassan Mosque, built in 1356.

▼ A priest holds the Cross of St. Mark, who is the patron saint of the Coptic religion. The Copts are descendants of the pharaonic Egyptians and still use a variation of the ancient language in their liturgy.

One God

The principal belief of Islam is the existence of one God, the same God worshipped by Christians and Jews, whom the Muslims call Allah. Islam means submission. Muslim means one who submits to monotheism as interpreted by the religion's founder, Mohammed (570-632 A.D.).

To be a Muslim, it is only necessary to say once in one's life, "There is no god but Allah. Mohammed is the Prophet of Allah". In fact, the devout repeat this submission five times a day, while prostrate and facing Mecca. They hope that these might be the last words they have on their lips when they die.

Mohammed

Mohammed was a merchant in Arabia. He often contemplated in the desert and at the age of 40 had a vision of the angel Gabriel who commanded him to proclaim monotheism to the pagan Arabian tribes. In Arabic, "to proclaim" is "Qur'an", and so the Koran (Holy Book) is the word of Allah as given to Mohammed.

The merchants of Mecca, concerned by the unsettling effects of this new religion, drove Mohammed out of the city in 622 A.D. His flight (the *hegira*) to Medina, where Islam first took root, is the event from which the Islamic calendar begins. The Christian year 1976 would be 1396 in an Islamic country like Egypt.

A tolerant religion

Though Islam spread throughout the Middle East and across North Africa by conquest, it usually treated other religions with tolerance. Egypt's profoundly religious Muslims represent 90 per cent of the population. The remaining 10 per cent are freely practising Copts, an early offshoot of orthodox Christianity. Once the dominant religious group in the country, many Copts converted to Islam, but those who remain Christians continue to play an important role in Egyptian life.

▼ Muslims go to mosques not only to pray, but to learn, read the newspapers, sleep, or have a chat. The atmosphere is informal and people of all backgrounds rub shoulders as brothers.

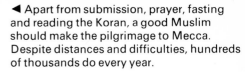
◄ Apart from submission, prayer, fasting and reading the Koran, a good Muslim should make the pilgrimage to Mecca. Despite distances and difficulties, hundreds of thousands do every year.

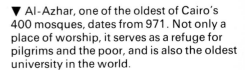
▼ Al-Azhar, one of the oldest of Cairo's 400 mosques, dates from 971. Not only a place of worship, it serves as a refuge for pilgrims and the poor, and is also the oldest university in the world.

◄ Traditionally, the *azan* (call to prayer) is made by the *muezzin* from a minaret. Loudspeakers on the minarets now save the *muezzin's* breath. The loudspeakers are linked to microphones or tape recorders below.

▼ El Mouallaqa, a Coptic church in Old Cairo, dates back to the fourth century. The Holy Family, fleeing from Herod, is believed to have stayed in Old Cairo which then, as now, had a Jewish community.

Custom and superstition

Egypt has undergone revolutionary changes over the past 20 years or so. But in a country of such age, it is not surprising that old traditions still flourish. The majority of the population still works on the land, and the rhythm of life has for so long followed the regime of the Nile.

Sham El Nassim Day, celebrating the advent of spring, can be traced back to pharaonic times. Families go out into their fields and gardens early in the morning and eat salted fish, onions and coloured eggs. The fish and onions are said to prevent disease, while the eggs symbolize life.

Religion is completely interwoven with everyday life and Islam is a great storehouse of custom. But it is also the enemy of primeval superstitions. The Evil Eye, the envious glance of almost any passer-by, is believed to be attracted by an immodest show of wealth, achievement, or beauty, and can harm or bewitch. Reciting certain verses from the Koran is one way of warding it off.

▲ Tradition is strong in the area of manners. A grown man, with children of his own, cannot smoke a cigarette in the presence of his father, out of respect.

▶ Dervishes are members of Muslim orders dedicated to lives of poverty and chastity. Some whirl, others howl, in their religious acts.

▼ The days are hot, but desert nights can be very cool. A cap or cloth on the head and the long, loose-fitting *djellaba* protect the body from extremes.

◀ Egyptian weddings are a major event and are as lavish as can be afforded. Flowers and gowns bloom in abundance. Bands play to the gyrations of bellydancers.

▼ Handprints of children are often seen on walls. This is one of the ways in which Egyptians hope to avert the Evil Eye.

▼ Many simple Egyptians believe that the Nile has magical properties. Despite the risk of disease, many Egyptians continue drinking from it, although piped water supplies are available.

▲ *Uzait Horu*, the Eye of Horus, is usually found on amulets worn to ensure safety and happiness. Even as Egypt modernizes, its traditional beliefs keep pace.

▼ The revolution taught Egyptians to determine their own destiny. But the old fatalism dies hard and "inshallah", meaning "Allah wills it", is often still heard.

▲ Time is one thing Egypt has a lot of, so much so that its passing often seems meaningless. Most Egyptians, except perhaps the younger generation, cannot be hurried.

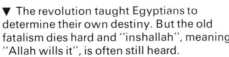

Family life

The traditional family

In a modern city like Cairo, the tone of family relationships is similar to that in the West. It is in the countryside that the old ways linger on.

The wife plays a submissive role to her husband, putting him before all else, even children. A proverb says, "Easier to have more children than to get another provider". While a man works in the fields, spends his evenings round a fire talking and smoking with his friends, and occasionally goes on trips beyond the village, his wife remains tied to the home and the children. To ensure absolute respect from his children, a father keeps emotionally distant from them. It is for the mother to give them tenderness, warmth and intimacy. But a wife is also mistress of her own household. She keeps the keys and legal documents and has control over the money.

Marriage

Islam permits a man to have up to four wives, but in modern Egypt no more than one man in a hundred has more than one wife.

According to Islamic law, a husband can divorce his wife simply by saying "I divorce thee" three times. Yet the divorce rate is lower in Egypt than it is in Britain. For both men and women, marriage is the most important event in their lives. It extends the range of relatives willing to provide assistance when needed.

An average urban family budget

Food, tea, coffee 40%

Housing, fuel, lighting 30%

Clothing and footwear 10%

Transport 10%

Durable household goods 10%

▶ While the men are labouring in the fields, their wives must tend to the village and household chores. Here a group of women are threshing corn. The daily round in the countryside is very hard in the almost complete absence of machines.

▲ Here at Giza, just outside Cairo, the Pyramids loom over the simple houses of people who are only half absorbed into urban ways. Some of them may work in the city, others may cater to tourists, but many still work on the nearby fields.

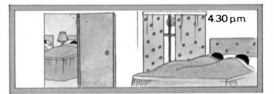

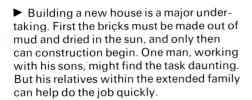

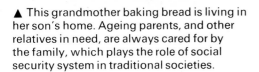

▲ This grandmother baking bread is living in her son's home. Ageing parents, and other relatives in need, are always cared for by the family, which plays the role of social security system in traditional societies.

► Building a new house is a major undertaking. First the bricks must be made out of mud and dried in the sun, and only then can construction begin. One man, working with his sons, might find the task daunting. But his relatives within the extended family can help do the job quickly.

Education and industrialization

Egypt is still a predominantly agricultural country which cannot grow enough food to feed its expanding population. It is looking towards rapid industrialization as an important contribution to solving its problems.

Because the government pays for all education, it feels justified in directing children to study the subjects it feels the country most needs. The school leaving age is 12 but is soon to be raised to 15. Many students in the cities are now sent to new vocational and industrial training centres. In the countryside Combined Rural Centres act as craft schools, as well as ante-natal and preventive medicine clinics.

Despite the former lack of facilities, the limited tax base and high military expenditure, Egypt has found the money to develop its educational system at an amazing rate. Since the 1952 revolution, the government has built nearly two schools every three days. In the past, only a fortunate few got an education, and most of those completing their courses became journalists, lawyers and civil servants, who, though perhaps useful, could not add to the productive base of the country. Now education is universal and is producing more skilled workers, technicians and scientists. The success of the educational effort, however, has not yet been matched by industrial growth and there are large numbers of highly-trained and educated Egyptians who cannot find jobs appropriate to their abilities.

The emancipation of women

Egypt has gone a long way towards the emancipation of women. The veil, for example, is virtually unknown, and the number of women doctors, scientists, teachers and politicians is increasing.

Education has played a vital role in this process. Schools are co-educational, and though fewer girls advance beyond the minimum school-leaving age than boys, their number is growing as education weakens traditional attitudes.

Many educated women have in turn joined the fight against illiteracy and for further female emancipation by becoming school teachers. In 1966, seventy per cent of the population were still illiterate, but under the onslaught of universal education and female emancipation, this figure is now falling fast.

The Egyptian school system

Kindergarten.(age 4-6 years)

Vocational/industrial training centres.

Combined rural centres.

▲ During primary school, young Egyptians achieve literacy in their own language before passing on to preparatory school where English, and perhaps French, is learned. From then on, they are "streamed" into schools appropriate to their abilities and the nation's needs. Half those completing secondary school go on to university, one of the highest proportions in the world.

▼ Egyptian children attend primary school from the age of six to twelve and then go on to preparatory school until they are 15. Here they begin learning English, which is the second language of the educational system.

◄ The growth of the student population has been greater than the present number of universities can contend with. Thousands often pack into lecture halls.

▼ The country's need for more scientists has led to everyone, including girls, being encouraged to continue their studies further. Women are more emancipated in Egypt than in other Arab countries.

▼ The oldest of Egypt's five universities is Al-Azhar in Cairo, formerly a purely religious institution which was secularized by Nasser in 1961. Along with Koranic instruction, which attracts students from all over the Muslim world, it now offers a general education.

Primary school. (age 6-12 years)

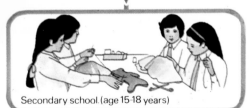

Preparatory school. (age 12-15 years)

Secondary school. (age 15-18 years)

University

Media and language

▲ The Rida Folklore Troupe has performed in Europe, the United States and the Soviet Union, and often appears on Egyptian television.

A social and political tool

Virtually all branches of the media are used by the government. The government is faced with the need to develop the country, to overcome illiteracy, to inform the populace and to inculcate the socialist principles of the revolution.

Radio and television are both state-owned, and broadcast nearly as many programmes as their counterparts in the most advanced Western countries. The government considers programmes to be part of the "liberation struggle" to promote socialism at home and to resist imperialism abroad. Cairo Radio broadcasts in over thirty different languages, concentrating especially on Black Africa while propaganda programmes like "Voice of the Arabs" are listened to throughout North Africa and the Middle East.

Audiences are huge, as much because of the high standard of Egyptian entertainment programmes as for any other reason. When meteorological conditions are right, Egyptian television can be picked up abroad and it is a testimony to its quality that people in Lebanon and Jordan sometimes specially equip their sets with the aerials to do so.

"Middle Arabic"

The problem of overcoming illiteracy is made greater by the difficulty that uneducated speakers of colloquial Arabic have in understanding the more complex classical Arabic of literature. The Egyptian media have adopted "middle Arabic", an innovation designed to bridge this gap. Through their pan-Arab influence, the media are promoting a social reform of profound significance.

▶ "Arabic numerals", as they are known in the West, had their origin in India. They reached us via the Arab world, where they look like this.

▼ Post boxes for local, country or foreign mail are distinguished from each other by colour and the appropriate symbol, as well as writing.

Arabic numerals

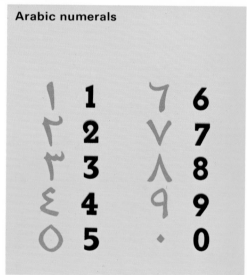

A selection of evening programmes on Egyptian television

Channel 5
5.00	Koran
5.05	Children's Corner
5.52	Evening Prayers
6.00	News
6.15	Athletics
6.45	European play
7.10	Prayers
7.12	European play (continued)
8.00	Around The World (series)
9.00	News
9.30	Stop, Who Are You?
10.00	The Girl and the Mercedes (Egyptian film)
11.30	Late news
11.35	Series from the Koran
11.45	Calling Oh Lord
12.00	Closedown

Channel 9
5.00	Koran
5.15	You And The World
5.30	French news
5.45	Film
6.00	European play (series)
6.45	News in English
7.00	World Animal Show
8.00	Events of the last 24 hours
8.25	Opera (series)
10.30	With Oum Khalthoum (singer)
11.30	Koran
11.45	Closedown

▲ Egyptians have a strong visual sense. Vividly pictorial advertising hoardings may appeal to the less literate, though even the Arabic calligraphy is highly elaborated for maximum effect.

▼ The diversity of reading material for sale on city streets is immense, and is said to be encouraged, rather than restricted, by state ownership of all newspapers, magazines and publishing houses.

▲ Egypt's cosmopolitan history and outlook is expressed by the common sight of signs in Arabic, English, French, and sometimes Russian. Education, commerce and television encourage the learning of foreign languages.

Eating the Egyptian way

A cosmopolitan cuisine

One of the legacies of the Ottoman Empire is a cuisine common to the entire Eastern Mediterranean. Kebab and moussaka are as familiar to Egyptians as they are to Greeks, while the small cup of thick, black coffee served at Cairo cafes is the same "Turkish coffee" served in Istanbul. French, Lebanese, Greek and Italian restaurants, and even American-style snack bars, are all found in Cairo and Alexandria. International influences are reflected in home cooking as well.

Typical Egyptian dishes

Mutton, buffalo and poultry are the central ingredients of many dishes. They are served with rich sauces, some on the sweet side, others highly spiced and perfumed with garlic, coriander and cloves.

The national dish is fool, prepared in a variety of inexpensive ways. Fool Medamis is the crushed fava bean mixed with cotton oil and served as a paste with salt and lemon juice added. Very rich in protein, it is eaten at any time of day, often with an egg on top at breakfast. During the month-long fast of Ramadan, Fool Medamis is traditionally eaten every evening.

A typical day's meals

▲ Breakfast is usually light, often only mint tea or coffee. It makes a quick start to an early working day.

▲ A mid-morning snack follows. It may consist of fool with a fried egg on top, unleavened bread and Turkish coffee.

▲ Lunch, in the mid-afternoon, is a major meal. Here it is stuffed pigeons, rice, salad, fruit and beer.

▲ An early evening snack might consist of tamiya (vegetable patties), tomato salad, olives, bread and lemon juice.

▲ Supper is eaten very late, after 10 p.m. Taheena (sesame seed paste), falafel (fried vegetable balls) and stuffed aubergines would be typical.

▲ Many Egyptians living in the cities have a light breakfast or lunch in a low-priced restaurant or cafe. Basic foods are cheap and a simple meal will often cost no more than the average bus ride.

Make yourself an Egyptian meal

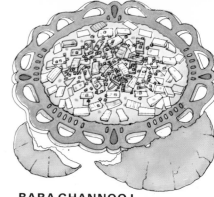

BABA GHANNOOJ
1 large aubergine
3 tablespoons fresh lemon juice
1 clove of garlic, chopped
1 teaspoon salt
2½ teaspoons olive oil
2 oz finely chopped onions
1 tablespoon finely chopped parsley

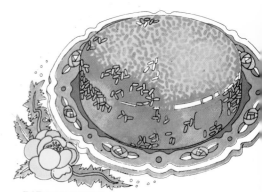

BIRAM RUZZ
2 oz softened butter
1 oz butter cut into pieces
1½ lbs long grain rice
2 lbs chicken cut into 6 pieces
½ pint of milk
½ pint double cream
1½ pints chicken stock

BASSBOUSSA
3 cups sugar, 3 cups semolina
3 level teaspoons baking powder
½ cup of milk
½ cup of yoghurt
1½ cups of water
2 tablespoons of butter
vanilla essence and lemon juice

Prick the aubergines in 3 or 4 places with the prongs of a long-handled fork. Then impale it on the fork and turn it over a gas flame until the skin chars and begins to split. If you have an electric stove, place the aubergine on a baking sheet and grill 4 inches from the heat for 20 minutes, turning it to char thoroughly.

When the aubergine is cool enough to handle, skin it, and cut away any badly charred spots on the flesh. Cut the aubergine lengthways and chop it finely. Mash the pulp to a smooth purée and beat in the lemon juice, garlic and salt to taste.

To serve, place the purée on a serving plate or pile it up in a bowl and sprinkle the top with the olive oil, chopped onions and parsley. Eat the Baba Ghannooj with flat bread.

Pre-heat the oven to Mark 6 (400°F). Butter a deep 5 pint casserole dish. Spread 10 oz of rice in the dish and cover with the chicken, adding salt and pepper. Boil the milk, cream and ¾ pint of stock and pour over the chicken. Spread the remaining rice on top and dot with pieces of butter. Bake uncovered for 15 minutes on the lowest oven shelf.

Meanwhile, simmer the remaining stock. Pour half of it into the casserole and bake for 15 minutes more. Pour in the remaining stock, transfer the casserole to the upper shelf, and bake for a further 30 minutes. Then remove the casserole, cover it tightly with a dish or foil, and let it rest at room temperature for 20 minutes.

To serve, run a knife around the edge of the casserole, and invert the dish to release the Biram Ruzz.

Mix one cup of sugar with the semolina. Dissolve the baking powder in the milk, and add it to the semolina and yoghurt. Put the mixture into a shallow 12 inch greased cake tin and bake on the middle shelf of a hot oven for 45 minutes, or an hour, until golden brown.

Meanwhile prepare the syrup. Dissolve two cups of sugar in the water, which should be on a very low heat. Then bring the water to the boil. Add one tablespoon of lemon juice and leave to boil for five minutes. Remove from heat and add one tablespoon of vanilla essence and two tablespoons of butter. Leave the syrup to cool.

When the cake is removed from the oven decorate the top with almonds, pour the syrup over it, and serve at once.

▼ Pigeons broiled on an open spit are a great Egyptian favourite. Sometimes they are caught in snares. More usually they are raised by the hundreds in specially constructed dovecotes.

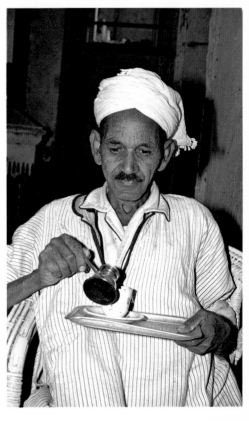

▲ The preparation and drinking of coffee is a ritual. Thick and black, Turkish-style, it is ordered according to the amount of sugar: sweet (*ziyada*), medium (*mazboota*), bitter (*saada*).

▲ Drinking water, mango juice, slices of coconut and other tidbits are sold in the streets. Street vendors are often landless fellahin who have left the countryside and have no other way of earning a living. In their case, they fulfil a need. Sometimes, however, there are beggars who sell a few paltry items which nobody really wants. In receiving payment, rather than charity, they maintain self-esteem.

The art of shopping

► Egypt has no supermarkets. Meats are usually sold on the day of slaughter because refrigeration is uncommon. For the same reason, most fruits and vegetables are sold fresh and are seasonal, though Egypt is developing a canning industry.

◄ The size and colour of Egyptian notes vary with their denomination. They are printed in English on one side, in Arabic on the other.

▲ Small shops, selling a variety of goods, line one of Cairo's busy streets. The great numbers of pedestrians often make it difficult for traffic to get through.

East meets West

In Egypt the traditional and the modern rub shoulders everywhere, and going shopping usually means rubbing shoulders with both. In a city like Cairo, going shopping can mean strolling along Kasr el Nil Street, lined with modern shops and department stores, or it can mean losing oneself in the labyrinthine passages of Khan el Khalili, an exotic oriental bazaar and the largest in the Middle East.

In the modern stores, as anywhere in the Western world, shopping is a straight-forward matter. Everything is under one roof, goods are very often pre-packaged and their prices are always fixed in advance.

Crafts and cunning

In Khan el Khalili, shopping is an adventure. Usually the goods are made right on the spot and the shopper can watch the craftsmen making jewellery, carving wood, and beating copperware. Each craft is found in its own area: leather goods on one street, glass on another, and perfumes and carpets each in separate sections of the bazaar. As one wanders along the streets and passage-ways, watersellers and cafes offer refreshment.

Everything is bargained over, a contest of wills which is half the pleasure of shopping. Browsing, bargaining, walking out, coming back and bargaining again can go on for hours. Everyone has plenty of time. During all this, the customer may well be offered the customary glasses of sweet mint tea.

Antiquities

A few dealers in Cairo, Luxor, and elsewhere, are licensed by the government to sell antiquities. *Ushabati*, human figures placed in ancient tombs to serve the deceased, are commonly available, as are scarabs, desert beetles made of stone or clay. However, most "antiquities" sold by the numerous unauthorized dealers are more likely to date from 1975 A.D. than from 1975 B.C.

▼ Mousky, the original and oldest commercial street in Cairo, runs through the heart of Khan el Khalili, an exotic cluster of *souks* teeming with milling crowds and mingled scents.

▲ Cotton is the major crop and Egypt is a major cotton manufacturing country. This shop can offer cotton and cotton goods of the very highest quality.

▲ Fool, taheena, and other basics of the housewife's weekly menu start here with the purchase of seeds, beans and grain direct from sacks on a street corner.

▶ When it comes to shopping in rural Egypt, East never encounters West at all. Here the village market supplies what range it can of meats, vegetables, fruits, grains, clothing and hardware goods.

Getting about in Egypt

The Ancient Highway

It is nearly impossible to look at any aspect of Egyptian life without again and again coming back to the Nile, and this is true of transport as well. The sight of giant sailing boats carrying tons of grain from one end of the country to the other, taking as long as a month to make the voyage, was as familiar to an ancient Egyptian as it is to Egyptians of the present day.

Virtually all cultivable land, and the villages, towns and cities are along the Nile Valley and in the Delta. Because of this, even modern forms of transport such as roads, railways and air routes, follow the age-old North-South axis.

Roads and Railways

Though adequate, Egypt's road system is not extensive and is not the primary means of transport. This is due to the convenience of river transport and the early development of the railway network under British rule. The railway network runs from Alexandria and from the Suez Canal through Cairo to Aswan. Trucks and railway wagons carry long-distance freight, though donkeys and camels are still familiar beasts of burden in rural areas.

▲ Ramses Square is the transportation hub of Cairo. The railway station links the capital with the major cities. Overloaded buses carry their burden of rush-hour passengers to and from work.

▼ Animals are still used as a major means of locomotion in Egypt. The donkey is the most common, though as many as 200,000 dromedaries serve the transport needs of fellahin, especially in Upper Egypt.

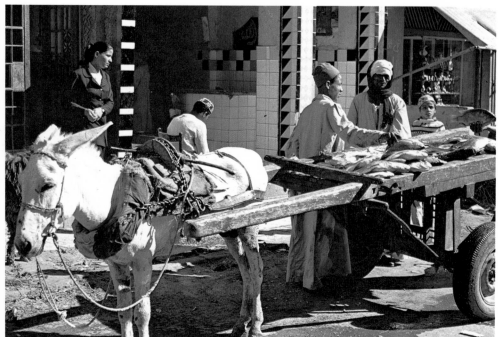

▲ Cairo's population of 8 million has 6,000 buses, of which only 2,000 are in working order. Standing room inside can be a luxury for those used to clinging on outside.

▶ The task of fetching water from the Nile falls to fellah women. A ring of cloth is placed on the head to take the weight and help balance the heavy pot.

▼ Egyptair is Egypt's national airline. It flies American and Russian aircraft on both internal and international routes. Air travel particularly is suitable in the Middle East.

مصر للطيران

EGYPTAIR

◀ *Feluccas* are the traditional form of transport along the Nile. Passenger carrying paddle-steamers now sail upriver to Luxor and Aswan.

▲ Egyptians are proud of the modern Hungarian diesels, painted in Egypt's national colours, which are assigned to express runs.

Living on the land

Along the river

Nearly two-thirds of the Egyptian population are *fellahin* (peasants) whose lives are intimately bound up with their lands along the Nile. Until the new High Dam finally checked the annual floods in 1967, the fellahin lived in small, closely clustered houses built on mounds beyond reach of the flood level. Now their villages can spread across lower ground, but the houses remain very small, often having no more than one room for a large family.

The fellahin use primitive devices such as the *sakiya* (buckets attached to a wheel driven by circling oxen) to lift the water onto the fields. There is also an intricate network of canals. The land is very fertile, and yields several harvests a year as the reward of unceasing labour. The fellahin cannot be idle if they are to feed themselves and their country.

As it is, the growth in population is out-stripping the food supply, and Egypt's most urgent need is to develop new land. By regulating and distributing the Nile's flow, the High Dam is increasing the supply of cultivable land by a third. Wells, some as deep as one mile, are raising water to the desert surface where the New Valley, in the Western Desert, is coming to life. The western limits of the Delta are being extended by the creation of the newly-fertile Liberation Province.

Deserts and oases

No more than 400,000 people live in Sinai or the Eastern or Western Deserts, whether as nomads or oasis-dwellers. Dates and olives are the major oasis crops, but so far only marginally contribute to Egypt's overall agricultural output. The nomadic desert tribes of Arab or Berber stock live mainly on the land, though some also live by trade or handicrafts.

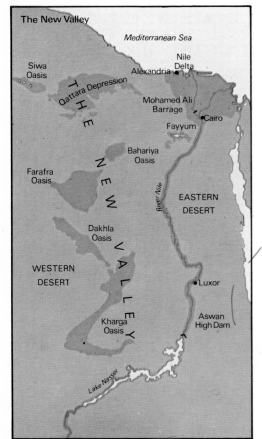

The New Valley map, showing: Mediterranean Sea, Siwa Oasis, Qattara Depression, Alexandria, Nile Delta, Mohamed Ali Barrage, Cairo, Fayyum, Bahariya Oasis, Farafra Oasis, THE NEW VALLEY, Dakhla Oasis, WESTERN DESERT, EASTERN DESERT, River Nile, Luxor, Kharga Oasis, Aswan High Dam, Lake Nasser

▲ Rain is almost unknown in Egypt, and so all water for the fields must come from the Nile or from subterranean wells. Mechanical pumps could do the work quickly and easily, but in a country as poor as Egypt most pumping work must be done by arduous human or animal labour, using age-old devices.

◄ The land is worked in much the same manner as it was in pharaonic times. This is a wooden plough, lacking the hard cutting edge of iron or steel. Fortunately the earth is soft and the plough does not break, but the work is hard nonetheless. The rich soil yields as many as five harvests a year, but only if the fellahin till and irrigate their land without ceasing.

◄ Most Bedouin are pastoral nomads who eke out their existence in the desert. They live in the simplest of huts or in tents. They are only a small minority in Egypt.

▼ The work is hard, but this fellah's land is his own. Many fellahin still do not possess land of their own and must work for others until new lands are reclaimed from the desert.

▼ Egypt's major crop is cotton, which is grown mostly in the Delta. Cultivated since ancient times and continually improved, it is the finest cotton in the world.

▼ Dates are Egypt's commonest fruit. Whole oases are given over to their cultivation. But they earn only a small proportion of the country's agricultural income.

▲ Maize production has steadily expanded. It has now become another major crop in Egypt's increasingly specialized agriculture.

Cairo, the dominant city

Strategic capital

The first stone of the Arab city was laid by Egypt's Fatimid conquerors on 5 August, 969 A.D., when the planet Mars was in the ascendant. The city took its name, al-Qahira, The Triumphant, from the warrior planet.

The Arabic al-Qahira is more familiar to us as Cairo, the city crucially situated at the apex of the Delta. Whoever possesses Cairo controls the Delta to the north and the long Nile Valley running southwards. Cairo is the fulcrum of power, the true capital of Egypt.

Mother of the World

Misr is the other name Egyptians have for their capital. Of the two, it is emotionally the more important. Misr is also the name for all Egypt, and the identification between capital and country is appropriate. Not only does the city politically and geographically dominate the country, but it is also swollen with people from every part of Egypt. An Egyptian abroad who says "I am going to Misr" means he is returning to Egypt. If he says the same thing in Alexandria, he means he is returning to Cairo. In either case, "going to Misr" carries the sense of going home. For the fellahin, Cairo is *Misr um al-dunya*: Misr, Mother of the World.

Cairo stands between the desert and the river. With its 8 million population, it is the largest Arab and African city. Politically, it is an important capital of the "Third World". The soul of Cairo is that of a sprawling *caravanserai*, or wayside inn, with the scent of glowing coals and musk and an astonishing variety of visitors from all over the Arab, Asian and African world. Cairo stands at the crossroads of the world.

Things to see in Cairo

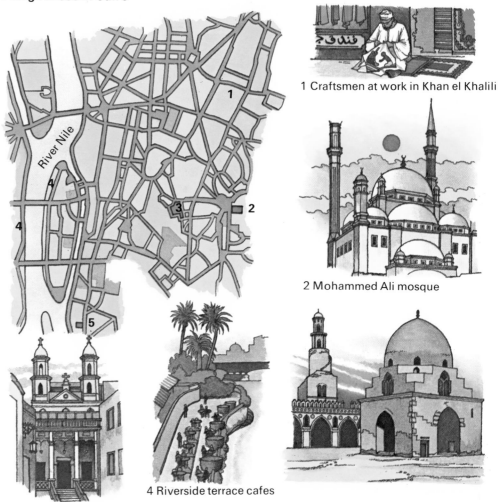

1 Craftsmen at work in Khan el Khalili

2 Mohammed Ali mosque

4 Riverside terrace cafes

5 Coptic church of El Mouallaqa

3 Ibn Tulun mosque

◄ From the top of the Cairo Tower, the city is seen straddling the Nile. Since Menes united Egypt and founded Memphis as his capital, there has been a city on or near this site at the apex of the Delta.

► Tahrir Square is the hub of modern Cairo. Major shopping and business streets radiate from it. The view is from the Hilton Hotel which overlooks the square in one direction, the Nile in the other.

▼ The Cairo Tower, 187 metres (613 ft) tall, is the city's modern landmark. Its design is based on the ancient lotus flower motif. A revolving restaurant at the top turns a full circle every half hour.

► The late afternoon sunlight bathes Old Cairo in warm orange tones. Amidst the warren of narrow streets are a jumble of traditional houses, old mosques, Coptic churches dating back to the first few centuries after the birth of Christ, and a synagogue.

Land of the pharaohs

▼ In Egyptian religion, death was not an end to life, but the transition to life everlasting. Here, a pharaoh of the XXth Dynasty meets Isis, Goddess of Heaven and Earth. The cult of Isis later flourished in Hellenistic times and was an early rival to, and influence upon, Christianity. Osiris, husband of Isis, was slain by the God of Darkness but was avenged by his son Horus and came back to life. The sufferings of Isis, and her joy upon her husband's resurrection, made her a sympathetic figure of worship.

Stability and prosperity

For nearly three thousand years, from the unification of Upper and Lower Egypt by Menes, to 332 B.C. when Alexander the Great conquered the country, Egypt was ruled by a long line of pharaohs. There were 330 pharaohs in all. Agriculture underpinned the country's prosperity, and discoveries of gold supplemented it. An efficient system of administration and taxation kept power and wealth firmly in the hands of the central authority, and a powerful army protected, and often extended, Egypt's frontiers.

The mood was of stability and continuity, rather than change. Popular insurrection was unknown. Pharaonic Egypt was the conservative state *par excellence*.

The good life

Art throughout this period emphasised the good life that was the prerogative of royalty and aristocracy. Religion projected the pleasures of life into an eternity that was attained once one had passed through the

▲ Akhenaten, with his wife Nefertiti, believed in one god, Aten, represented by the sun disk. Akhenaten was a philosopher and poet, and encouraged realism in art.

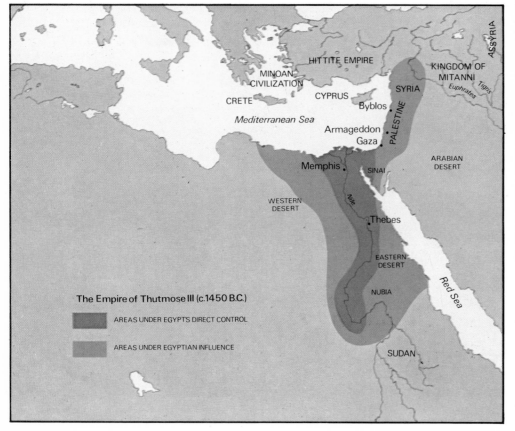

The Empire of Thutmose III (c. 1450 B.C.)

▮ AREAS UNDER EGYPTS DIRECT CONTROL

▮ AREAS UNDER EGYPTIAN INFLUENCE

◄ The ancient Egyptian Empire reached its greatest extent in the fifteenth century B.C. when Thutmose III conquered Syria and Palestine.

ceremony of death. The attainment of eternity was as simple as crossing over to the west bank of the Nile, where the sun set and where the pyramids and other great tombs were constructed.

The Egyptian Empire

Of many of the pharaohs, little is known except for a few inscriptions, the occasional monument, and sketchy records of battles fought. Thutmose III (died 1447 B.C.) stands out in history as the world's first empire-builder. Egypt always felt threatened by the ambitions of the numerous city-kings of Palestine and Syria. When these kings rose in revolt against Egyptian influence in the area, the Egyptian army, led by Thutmose, decisively beat them at Armageddon. Thutmose reorganised his conquered territories, and raised two obelisks at Heliopolis to proclaim his prowess. One, known as Cleopatra's Needle, now stands on the Embankment in London, the other in New York's Central Park.

▲ Hunting was a traditional part of royal life. Pharaohs were often depicted shooting arrows at lions from their chariots. Here the scene is more tranquil. The pharaoh floats through the Delta waters while a specially-trained cat flushes out ducks.

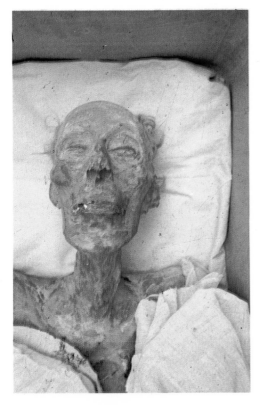

▲ The Egyptians were unsurpassed in the art of mummification. The mummy of Ramses II (a contemporary of Moses) lies intact in the Cairo Museum.

▶ The temple at Karnak was extended and embellished by pharaohs over the course of 2,000 years. It is more spectacular than even Cecil B. de Mille's epic film sets.

Arab conquerors and Turkish overlords

Greek learning as Alexandria, Islam fell heir to Hellenism, which it helped to transmit to the West.

The Arabs translated Greek works on science, philosophy, mathematics and medicine. They invented trigonometry and algebra (deriving from the Arabic *al-jabr*, meaning the reunion of broken parts).

One of the greatest men of this period was Al-Biruni (973-1048), physician, astronomer, mathematician, physicist, chemist, geographer and historian—a profound and original scholar. Later, Ibn Khaldun (1332-1406) began to interpret history, rather than just narrating it. He was acknowledged as the greatest historian of the Middle Ages.

The Arab explosion

Following the death of Mohammed in 632 A.D., Islam expanded as a religious and political force under a succession of remarkably able caliphs. By the middle of the eighth century, Arab armies had swept west to the Atlantic, north to Poitiers in France, and east to India.

Egypt was conquered as early as 642. The Copts, already in rebellion against the orthodox Christianity of their nominal rulers in Constantinople, welcomed the Arabs as liberators. The Arabs permitted them to practise Christianity as they liked, and found them indispensable in positions of finance and administration.

The Golden Age

The first centuries of empire were a Golden Age of Arab power and cultural achievement. The Arabs drew upon the talents of Christians, Jews, Zoroastrians and pagans. Through conquering such great centres of

New masters from the east

In the eleventh century the Seljuk Turks arose out of Asia and adopted Islam en route. They sacked Baghdad and installed themselves as caliphs. The Arab Empire, which had been disintegrating, was finished, but Islam was revitalized in time to ward off the threat of the Crusades. This movement, like Islam itself, had imperialist as well as religious motives.

The Crusaders seized the Holy Land and set their sights on Egypt. The great hero and defender of Islam was a Seljuk officer, Salal al-Din (Saladin), who created a Syrian-Egyptian empire and threw the Christians out of Palestine.

For the moment, Egypt was strong, but under the increasingly heavy hand of first Seljuk, and then Ottoman Turkish rule, it was to slumber for nearly 800 years.

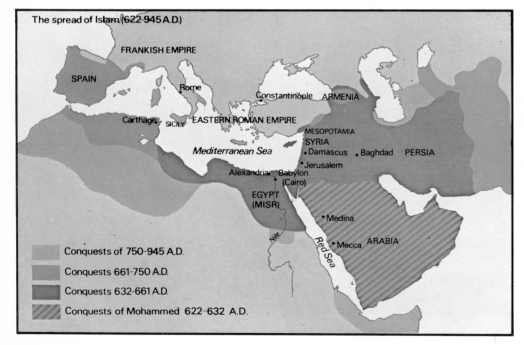

The spread of Islam (622-945 A.D.)

FRANKISH EMPIRE

SPAIN

Rome

Carthage · SICILY · EASTERN ROMAN EMPIRE

Constantinople · ARMENIA

Mediterranean Sea

MESOPOTAMIA
SYRIA
· Damascus · Baghdad PERSIA
· Jerusalem

Alexandria · Babylon (Cairo)

EGYPT (MISR)

Nile · Red Sea

· Medina

· Mecca ARABIA

Conquests of 750-945 A.D.
Conquests 661-750 A.D.
Conquests 632-661 A.D.
Conquests of Mohammed 622-632 A.D.

▲ After seizing Jerusalem and the rest of Palestine, Richard the Lionheart and his Crusaders aimed at conquering Egypt. But Saladin stopped the Christians in their tracks, and recovered the Holy Land for Islam.

◀ The oldest mosque in Cairo was built by Ibn Tulun, a Turkish slave of the Arab caliph in Baghdad. Tulun was sent to Egypt to act as governor, but made the country independent in 868 A.D.

▼ Mohammed, the founder of Islam, is considered by Muslims to be one of a long line of God's prophets that has included Moses and Jesus.

MAHOMETH

AVICENNA
ex Codice antiqvo Galeni.

▲ While Europe slept through its Dark Ages, Islam sparkled with genius. Avicenna, known as Ibn Sina, (980-1037 A.D.) was one of the greatest physicians of the time. He is mentioned by Chaucer in *The Canterbury Tales*. In medicine, the Arabs did not alter the basic theory of the Greeks, but enriched it by practical observation and clinical experience.

▶ Saladin overthrew the Fatimid Arab rulers of Egypt who had allowed the country to grow weak. He built his Citadel against the Moqqattam Hills overlooking Cairo, where 800 years later Mohammed Ali built his mosque.

The awakening

Mameluke misrule

The Mamelukes, a caste of Turkish warrior slaves, were introduced into Egypt by Saladin. In time, they became masters of the country. They lived in luxury at the expense of the people. The cities were derelict. Irrigation was neglected. The population, only one quarter of what it had been in pharaonic times, had sunk into the fatalistic attitude of a subject race. The country suffered further when the new sea-route to India around Africa stole trade away from Egyptian caravans.

So far as the outside world was concerned, at the end of the eighteenth century Egypt and all her history were like a closed book. She slumbered, inaccessible and without interest.

Napoleon in Egypt

In 1798 Napoleon was only 28, a visionary with dreams of emulating Alexander, but also a practical general who knew that a canal cut across the isthmus of Suez could help him seize India from Britain. Nelson's victory at the Battle of the Nile forced Napoleon to withdraw. But the venture put Egypt back on the map, and opened Egypt's eyes to the modern world.

Mohammed Ali

When Napoleon departed, both the Turkish army and the dispossessed Mamelukes returned. Mohammed Ali, an Albanian soldier in the service of the Sultan, played Sultan and Mamelukes off against each other, establishing himself as pasha of an Egypt which was only nominally subject to Ottoman control.

Mohammed Ali admired Napoleon. He believed in Western ideas and technology, and welcomed European traders and engineers. He introduced cotton from India, initiated modern irrigation, redistributed land and established Western-style schools. His grandson Ismail presided over the construction of the Suez Canal, which brought Egypt back to the centre of world trade, but brought the British to Egypt too.

▲ Mohammed Ali (1769-1849) began the modernization of Egypt. He founded a dynasty which lasted until Farouk was overthrown by Nasser in 1952.

► Napoleon's expedition to Egypt was as much scientific as military. He enquired into history, irrigation and agriculture, and introduced Egypt's first printing press.

◀ In 1811, Mohammed Ali invited the Mamelukes to dinner. He then sent them home through a narrow street, where he massacred them with his troops. In this way he became absolute ruler of Egypt.

▲ During their occupation of Egypt, the British helped modernize the irrigation system. They built the original dam at Aswan in 1902, now superseded by the Soviet-built High Dam.

▲ De Lesseps built the Suez Canal but the British were soon running it, and Egypt as well. Lord Cromer, above, was *de facto* ruler of Egypt from 1883 to 1907.

▶ The Suez Canal was completed in 1869. Cairo was redesigned, the Opera House opened, and Verdi commissioned to write *Aïda* to celebrate the occasion.

Legends
and heroes

The search for identity

For over 2,000 years, until very recently, Egypt was ruled by foreigners who often used her to further their foreign ambitions.

Cleopatra was a Greek who dreamt of a Greco-Roman empire. Ibn Tulun was a Turk, Saladin a Kurd, Mohammed Ali an Albanian. For Lord Cromer, the Suez Canal was the British Empire's lifeline to India.

Many of the great figures in Egyptian history have not been Egyptians at all. The country has sometimes benefited from their rule, but for modern Egyptians it is easier to revere leaders who have sprung from Egyptian soil, and who have given Egypt back to the Egyptians.

Yet Arabi, Zaghloul, Mustafa Kamel and Nasser must share the spotlight with poets, singers and characters out of popular tales, for Egyptians thrive as much on passion as on pride.

▲ Portraits of Nasser, sometimes stern, more often smiling, are often seen in Egyptian streets and public buildings. As the first native-born leader of an independent Egypt in nearly 2,500 years, his memory is a source of great pride.

Cleopatra

Though she was a foreigner, Egyptians have accepted Cleopatra as the symbol, or trademark, of a romantic view of their past. Elizabeth Taylor provided the world with its most recent image of Cleopatra. From coins of the time it is clear that her appeal to men like Caesar and Antony must have been more in her character and power than in any overwhelming beauty.

▲ Oum Khalthoum, the Egyptian singer, was immensely popular throughout the Arab world. Her performances could outdraw any appearance by Nasser, and at her funeral in 1975, millions wept in the Cairo streets.

▶ In 1882, the fellah officer Arabi failed in his nationalist uprising against Ismail, a stooge of European imperialism. Afterwards the British took direct control of Egypt. Where Arabi failed, Nasser later triumphed.

◀ Pharaonic gods possessed both human and animal attributes. Anubis (centre), god of the dead, is represented with a jackal's head, suggesting swiftness of movement. Hathor is on the left, Osiris on the right. The animals identified with the gods were themselves considered sacred.

Anubis

Hathor

Osiris

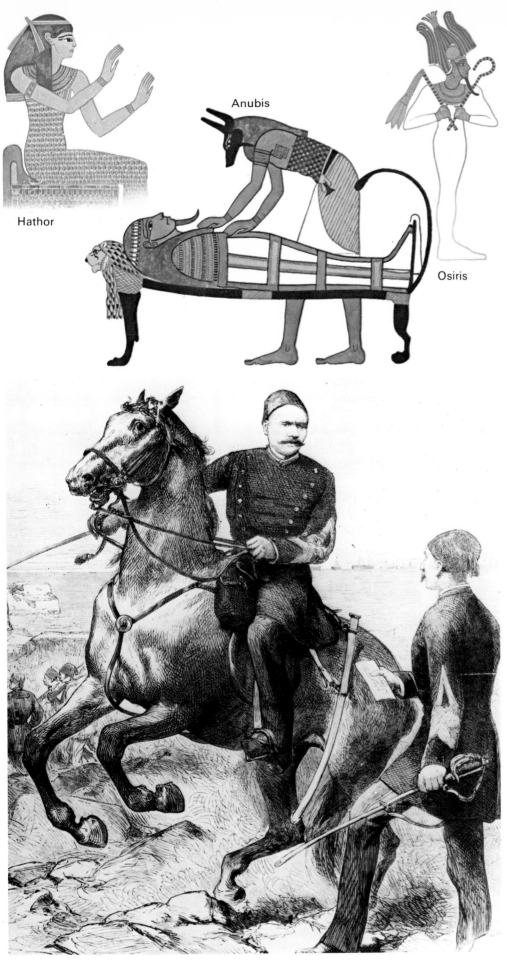

▼ Betrayed by his first wife, King Shahr Yar married another woman every day, killing her the next morning. But the beautiful Scheherazade told him such wonderful tales each night that he would spare her life for yet another day. The tales are famous throughout the world as the *Thousand and One Nights*.

Sports and leisure

Outdoor sports

A great variety of sports familiar throughout the world are enjoyed by spectators and participants in Egypt too. Tennis, golf, riding, rowing, sailing, water skiing, hunting and fishing are among them. But the most popular sport at the moment is football, and nearly every male Egyptian has played the game at one time or another during his life.

Swimming is swiftly gaining in popularity, however. Most clubs in the cities have swimming pools, and children train in the sport from an early age. Swimming is well on the way to becoming the national sport and already Egypt is doing very well in international contests.

Diverse entertainments

When going out for an evening's entertainment, a Cairene might well go to the city's specially-built puppet theatre, the largest in the world. Puppet shows are a traditional form of entertainment but are losing ground to films.

The Egyptian film industry is the largest in the Middle East and has produced many notable actors and directors such as Omar Sharif. But young Egyptians find many of these films too romantic, so American action films are gaining in popularity.

Poetry has always occupied a major place in Arab culture and today it is the singers, heirs of the poets, who are the heroes of the Arab world. The late Oum Kalthoum was the best loved, but others are indulged. Abdel Wahhab so prizes his throat that he never goes out without a cloth over his mouth, while Farid al Atrash, a Druse prince from the Lebanon, has a Cairo skyscraper named after him.

▲ After work, men gather at cafes to talk and smoke and have a game of "trick-track". Known to us as backgammon, its place of origin is uncertain, but a board dating back to 3000 B.C. has been found in the Nile Valley.

► Belly dancing is enjoyed by Egyptians of both sexes. It is performed not only in nightclubs, but at family occasions such as weddings. Most girls from the age of six upwards know how to belly dance.

▲ Pole fighting is a harmless, but tough sport played by the fellahin. It offers an exciting contrast to routine field labour.

◄ Each year the Cairo police challenge Oxford, Cambridge, Harvard and Yale to a boat race. The Cairo police usually win.

▼ El Shafei is one of Egypt's outstanding tennis players. Local and international tournaments take place throughout the year.

▲ During the hottest summer months, Alexandria, with its cool sea breezes and fine sandy beaches, becomes a playground for Egyptian holidaymakers. The atmosphere is more Mediterranean than oriental.

Preserving Egypt's past

Ignorance and destruction

When Napoleon arrived in Egypt with 175 artists, scholars and scientists he found the Pyramids and Sphinx, at Giza, half buried in the sands. The past had been neglected and knowledge of it was slight.

During the years of Turkish rule, the Pyramids were regarded as nothing more than a convenient supply of building stone for new palaces and mosques in Cairo. Saladin entirely demolished several smaller pyramids to construct his Citadel with their stones.

Curiosity and science

The French expedition opened Egypt up to curious European eyes. Champollion deciphered the Rosetta Stone and thereby found the key to the understanding of ancient Egyptian hieroglyphics. Monuments, temples and tombs acquired meaning through the understanding of their inscriptions. Pharaonic history lay revealed, and Egypt became the world's largest outdoor museum.

The Englishman, Flinders Petrie, established the method for scientific excavations in the 1880s which saved many sites from the ruinous methods of amateurs. Egyptian insistence that Egyptian treasures go to the Cairo Museum put a stop to cultural "looting" by foreign museums.

Progress and preservation

The development needs of modern Egypt have sometimes conflicted with the desire to preserve her ancient past. The completion of the High Dam at Aswan threatened to drown Abu Simbel beneath the rising waters of a huge artificial lake. An international team of engineers, financed by UNESCO, managed to raise the temple to higher ground before it was submerged. This exercise in international cooperation showed that the preservation of Egypt's past is the responsibility of the entire world.

▲ The hand-sawn sections of the temples and colossi of Abu Simbel await reconstruction on higher ground.

▼ Pompey's Pillar is one of the few reminders of Alexandria's Roman past. Even less survives from Ptolemaic times.

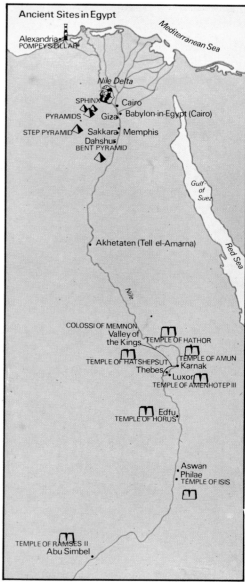

Ancient Sites in Egypt

Mediterranean Sea

Alexandria
POMPEY'S PILLAR

Nile Delta

SPHINX
PYRAMIDS · Cairo
· Giza · Babylon-in-Egypt (Cairo)

STEP PYRAMID
Sakkara · Memphis
Dahshur
BENT PYRAMID

Gulf of Suez

Akhetaten (Tell el-Amarna)

Red Sea

Nile

COLOSSI OF MEMNON
Valley of the Kings
TEMPLE OF HATHOR
TEMPLE OF HATSHEPSUT
Thebes · Karnak
Luxor
TEMPLE OF AMENHOTEP III
TEMPLE OF AMUN

Edfu
TEMPLE OF HORUS

Aswan
· Philae
TEMPLE OF ISIS

TEMPLE OF RAMSES II
Abu Simbel

◀ After completion of the old Aswan Dam in 1902, the island of Philae was periodically flooded, only some of its pharaonic, Ptolemaic and Roman temples showing above water. Dutch engineers have now cut Philae off from the Nile with dykes, leaving it high and dry again.

▲ The Colossi of Memnon were guardians of the mortuary temple of Amenophis III at Thebes. They have suffered from extremes of temperature and human defacement. They were tourist attractions even in ancient times. Eight Roman governors of Egypt carved their names on the statues.

▲ Tutankhamun became a household name when his grave was discovered intact, its riches undisturbed by grave-robbers, a rare event of Egyptology. The young king was encased within three coffins, the innermost of solid gold, and wore this gold mask on his head.

◀ Glowing in the fierce sun, the rugged cliffs of the Libyan mountains opposite Karnak, serve as a backdrop to the Sanctuary of Hatshepsut, a pharaoh's widow who became the first female ruler of Egypt.

Revolution

▲ Saad Zaghloul was a nationalist leader after the First World War. He negotiated with the British for their withdrawal, but they maintained a force in the Canal Zone.

▼ Nasser was too poor to study law at university, and entered the Military Academy. At school he read biographies of Caesar, Gandhi, Napoleon and Voltaire.

Nasser's rise to power

Gamal Abdel Nasser was the successor to such nationalist heroes as Colonel Arabi and Saad Zaghloul in the struggle to free Egypt from foreign rule. Nasser was born in Alexandria, the son of a post office clerk from a rural village in Upper Egypt. Like many city-dwelling Egyptians of fellahin background, the Nasser family maintained close rural ties. Nasser's identification with the peasantry shaped his policies when he became the first true Egyptian leader of an independent Egypt in over 2,250 years.

After the Second World War, Nasser gathered round him a secret group of army officers who resented political corruption. In 1952 they led an army coup which overthrew King Farouk. Their immediate priority was land reform. Agricultural holdings were limited to 200 acres and rents were fixed at a level within reach of the ordinary peasant.

The Suez crisis

The government wanted to build a new dam at Aswan which would increase farming land by one-third, and went to Britain, France and the United States for loans. These were refused because of Nasser's willingness to deal with both East and West. This financial arm-twisting led Nasser to nationalize the Suez Canal Company in 1956. Its revenues, instead of draining to the West, would help finance the High Dam.

In response, Israel, France and Britain invaded Egypt. World opinion was outraged and the invaders were forced to withdraw. Nasser was left with both the Canal and a considerable moral victory.

Nasser now carried the revolution further. A limit was put on incomes; workers were given shares in their employers' companies; the banks and the cotton trade were nationalized, as were the 50 largest industrial concerns. Holdings in land were further reduced, releasing a million acres for redistribution.

The Six Day War

The Six Day War in June, 1967, was a blow to Egypt and to Nasser personally. Israel took Gaza, Sinai and the East Bank of the Canal. Nasser resigned but was called back by mass demonstrations. Nasser represented Arab pride and self-respect, and though the country could bear to lose a war, it could not lose the man who embodied those essential qualities. But in 1970 Nasser died and Egypt's fortunes were at a low ebb. The task facing Anwar Sadat, Egypt's new President, was formidable: to solve Egypt's pressing international and domestic problems.

◄ King Farouk was a fat playboy who enjoyed all the benefits of rule to excess, but did little for the millions of ordinary Egyptians. Overthrown by the revolution, he sailed away to Italy in his yacht.

▲ When they took power, the average age of the Revolutionary Command Council was 35, and they were all of fellah stock. Neguib, their nominal leader, and Nasser, their driving force, sit together at the centre. Sadat, who met Nasser at the Military Academy, is seated far right. Nasser later became President just before the Suez crisis.

▼ On 23 July 1952, after the failure of Farouk to satisfy nationalist protests, a group of young army officers seized power without bloodshed. They took over military headquarters and the radio stations, and together with their figurehead, the popular General Neguib, were given a triumphant reception in the streets.

▲ On 26 January 1952, rioting broke out in Cairo, in reaction to the shooting by British troops of a company of Egyptian police in the Canal Zone. The shooting marked the beginning of the revolution.

From crafts to industry

imported, or instead of being mass-produced in factories, they are made in the old pre-industrial way, by individual craftsmen in their own small workshops which often double as retail outlets.

For a poor country like Egypt, the importation of foreign goods means spending valuable money abroad when it could be put to better use in developing home industries. This would create jobs for Egyptians and earn money from foreign sales which would pay for the food imports Egypt needs to feed her rapidly expanding population.

▲ For more and more Egyptian men and women every year, the demands and benefits of industrialization bring a new way of life.

A shortage of energy

The industrial sector of the Egyptian economy is small, employing only about ten per cent of the work force. Lack of energy sources has been a major reason for the country's failure to develop as fast as other countries. All coal has had to be imported, though recent finds of both coal and oil will go some way towards alleviating the problem. Hydro-electric power from the High Dam has been Egypt's greatest hope for increasing the pace of industrialization. The search for new oil fields continues.

The need to export

Many manufactured goods have to be

New industries

Since the days of Mohammed Ali, Egypt's major area of industrial development has been in the textile industry, though the food processing industry ranks in second place.

Diversification has been encouraged since the 1952 revolution, however, and Egypt produces radios, televisions, cars and tractors. The establishment of the steel works at Helwan, just south of Cairo, has laid the foundation for the development of heavy industry. Chemical and fertilizer plants have been developed at Aswan. Revenue from the Suez Canal, which reopened in June, 1975, is providing capital for further industrial development.

▼ Egypt's ambition is to become the major industrial nation in the Middle East. The steel works at Helwan provide an essential foundation for developing heavy industry.

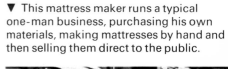

◀ Some tasks can never be industrialized. This engraver is one of the craftsmen who specialize in jewellery, woodwork, and other arts in Cairo's Khan el Khalili.

▼ This mattress maker runs a typical one-man business, purchasing his own materials, making mattresses by hand and then selling them direct to the public.

◀ Egypt has a large textile industry. But much of the transformation from cloth to clothing still occurs in simple workshops.

▼ Geometric inlay work in the Sultan Hassan mosque, in Cairo, is a superb example of traditional craftsmanship. Islam forbids the use of human or animal images.

Egypt's influence on the world

▶ Michel Shalhoub was born in Cairo in 1933. In 1964 he captained Egypt's Olympic bridge team and made his English-language acting debut in *Lawrence of Arabia*. He had by then changed his name to Omar Sharif.

▼ The Egyptians were the first to use columns and capitals, deriving their form from the trunks and bundles of stems used in earlier times. At Karnak the capitals are lotus flowers, the columns their stems.

Science and engineering

The annual flooding of the Nile, and the need to control it and use it to irrigate and fertilize the land, encouraged the ancient Egyptians to master engineering, astronomy and mathematics, and to keep regular and precise records.

The construction and maintenance of levees, dykes and canals required considerable organizational and engineering abilities. Posterity is most aware of these talents as applied to other projects, such as the Pyramids, which are near-perfect in their geometrical symmetry. They are so precisely aligned that archaeologists believe that sophisticated astronomy must have been used.

The solar calendar

The ancient Egyptians relied on a solar calendar of 365 days for the operation of a nationwide irrigation system and for knowing in advance when to hold the water back and when to release it. This calendar served as the prototype for the Julian calendar, of which ours is merely an adjusted version.

The foundations of knowledge

These achievements contributed to the body of learning which first developed in the Eastern Mediterranean lands. After the decline of the Hellenistic world, the Arabs fell heirs to this knowledge, and transmitted it centuries later to a Europe awakening from its Dark Ages. Just as schools in Alexandria and Cairo played a crucial role in the past, today Egypt is a major assimilator of ideas, and a training ground for skills which are returning again from the West to the developing Arab world.

Papyrus

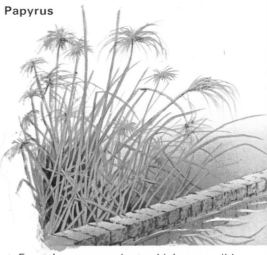

▲ From the papyrus plant, which grew wild in the Delta, the Egyptians made boats, cloth and sandals. They also used it to make a light-weight, flexible writing material.

▲ President Sadat talks with the late King Faisal of Saudi Arabia. Modern Egypt is the political cornerstone of the Arab world, the one country to which the others must in the end defer in matters of war and peace.

◄ Two of the Seven Wonders of the Ancient World were in Egypt: the Pharos Lighthouse in Alexandria Harbour, and the Pyramids at Giza, which, until modern times, were the highest structures in the world. They have still not been surpassed in height by any building of stone except Ulm Cathedral.

► Although the Egyptians did not invent writing, they did develop the first Mediterranean literature. Said a scribe to his son: ''Set your heart on being a scribe, for a book is of greater value than a house, more beautiful than a castle''.

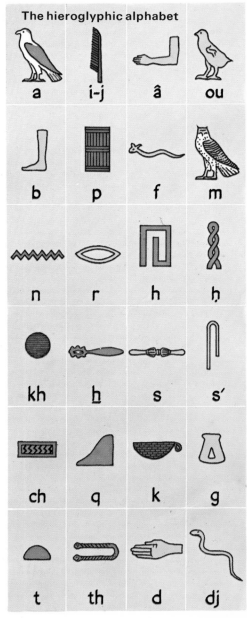

The hieroglyphic alphabet

a	i-j	â	ou
b	p	f	m
n	r	h	ḥ
kh	ẖ	s	s'
ch	q	k	g
t	th	d	dj

▲ The papyrus stems were cut into strips and laid out first horizontally, then crossed with a vertical layer. The strips were then beaten into a flat sheet and put out in the sun to dry.

▲ Sheets could be made into rolls which were easy to carry or store. Papyrus was used for thousands of years until paper, from China, was introduced by the Arabs.

How Egypt is changing

New confidence

The effect of the October 1973 war with Israel was to restore the pride Egypt lost after her humiliating June 1967 defeat. Now morale is high, and President Sadat, bolstered by popular support, is free to pursue policies of liberalization at home and innovation abroad.

Reconstruction and development

Twenty-five years of military confrontation have cost Egypt money and resources she can ill-afford. The moves towards peace, and help from rich Arab oil states, provide opportunities to industrialize and grapple with serious internal problems.

The Suez Canal has been cleared and re-opened. Suez, Ismailia and Port Said are being rebuilt. Here, and elsewhere in Egypt, the Ministry of Tourism is building hotels, developing new resorts, and improving the internal air services. Egypt hopes to attract five million visitors to the country each year. European and American contractors and banks are being involved.

Ensuring peace

The intention is to use the foreign money brought into Egypt to develop the country's economy, and to improve conditions for ordinary Egyptians. It is also hoped to involve the Western powers in Egypt's future so that never again could they afford to see Egypt damaged by war.

▲ Egypt is looking forward to a big tourist boom, which will pay for industrial development and improve living standards.

◄ Dr. Kissinger confers with President Sadat. Egypt is the spokesman for the Arab world. Her military victory, and the subsequent oil restrictions, forced America and Europe to revise outmoded attitudes.

▲ This sparkling new village of Kom Ombo is one of many built for Nubians, who were driven from their old settlements by the rising waters of Lake Nasser.

► Modern urban housing estates are part of Egypt's attempt to solve its problems of poverty, poor health, and a very rapidly expanding population.

▼ Madame Sadat visited troops at the front during the October 1973 war. Her presence was a gesture of gratitude to the soldiers who had crossed the Suez Canal and liberated a part of Sinai.

Reference
Human and physical geography

Temperature and rainfall

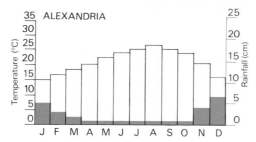

ALEXANDRIA

HELIOPOLIS (CAIRO)

Climate

Only a thin strip of the northern coastline of Egypt shares in a Mediterranean-type climate, giving Alexandria an annual rainfall of 177.8 mm (7 inches). Otherwise, Egypt is within the arid zone, with rainfall throughout most of the country well under 25.4 mm (1 inch) per year. There is no part of Egypt where agriculture is possible without the help of irrigation.

Temperatures increase from north to south in parallel with the aridity. The highest temperatures are usually recorded in spring, during the period of the *khamsin*, a hot, dry wind comparable to the *sirocco* of North Africa. The humidity throughout the whole of Egypt can then fall to under 2%.

Irrigation formerly depended on the Nile's annual rise between June and November, but since 1967 the river has been completely controlled by the new High Dam and water can be measured out throughout the year.

FACTS AND FIGURES

Official name: Arab Republic of Egypt (A.R.E.).

Position: Primarily in the north-east corner of Africa, though Sinai lies in Asia. Bordered by Israel, Libya and the Sudan, with the Mediterranean on its north coast, the Red Sea on its east coast.

Constituent parts: divided into 25 aministrative areas called *muhafazat*: Cairo, Alexandria, Port Said, Ismailia, Damietta, Suez, Mansura, Zagazig, Benha, Kafr esh-Sheikh, Tanta, Shibin el-Kom, Damanhur, Giza, Faiyum, Beni Suef, Minya, Asyut, Suhag, Qena, Aswan, the New Valley, the Red Sea, the Western Desert, and Sinai.

Area: 386,198 square miles.

Population: 37 million (estimated 1975).

Capital: Cairo.

Language: Arabic.

Religion: 90% Muslim, the remainder being primarily Coptic Christians, who are particularly numerous in Middle Egypt, south of Luxor in Upper Egypt, and in the larger Delta towns.

The State: Became a sovereign state in 1922. Officers' coup, engineered by Nasser, formally headed by General Neguib, in 1952. Proclaimed a republic in 1953. Syria and Egypt joined to become the United Arab Republic, 1958-61. Egypt became the Arab Republic of Egypt in 1971.

International organizations: The four major international organizations of which Egypt is a member are the Arab League, the Organization of Arab Petroleum Exporting Countries (OAPEC), the Organization of African Unity and the United Nations. Egypt also belongs to other United Nations organizations such as UNESCO, UNICEF, the World Health Organization and the Food and Agriculture Organization.

The natural vegetation of Egypt

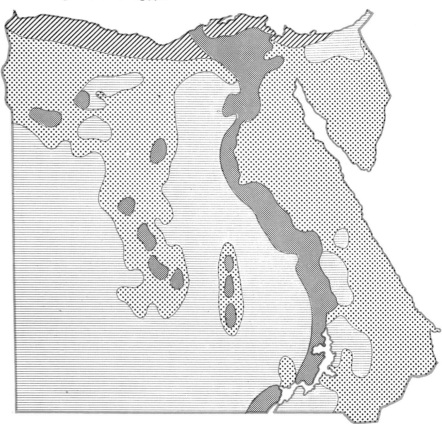

Dry Steppe & Desert Vegetation

Halfa Grass Steppe & Semi-desert

Desert Shrub

Sahara Sandy & Stony Desert

Forest Vegetation

Oases & Nile Valley

The population density

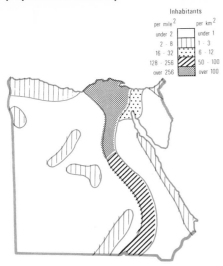

Inhabitants

per mile²	per km²
under 2	under 1
2 - 8	1 - 3
16 - 32	6 - 12
128 - 256	50 - 100
over 256	over 100

A rising population

Egypt's population at the last full census in 1960 was 26.08 million, but was estimated to be 37 million in 1975. It is growing at around 2.5 per cent a year. Although the birth rate has been falling, the death rate has fallen even more dramatically. This is a reflection of improved health services. The strain that rising population puts on Egypt's food supplies, housing and services is the country's greatest problem. 95% of the total population lives in that 6.6% of the country which is cultivable, and in that area Egypt is one of the world's most densely populated countries.

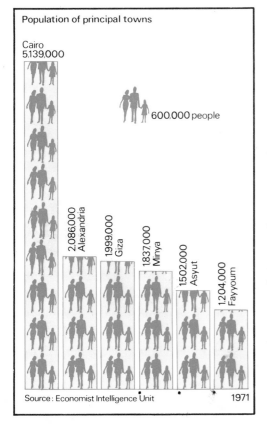

Population of principal towns

Cairo 5,139,000

600,000 people

2,086,000 Alexandria
1,999,000 Giza
1,837,000 Minya
1,502,000 Asyut
1,204,000 Fayyoum

Source: Economist Intelligence Unit   1971

The system of government

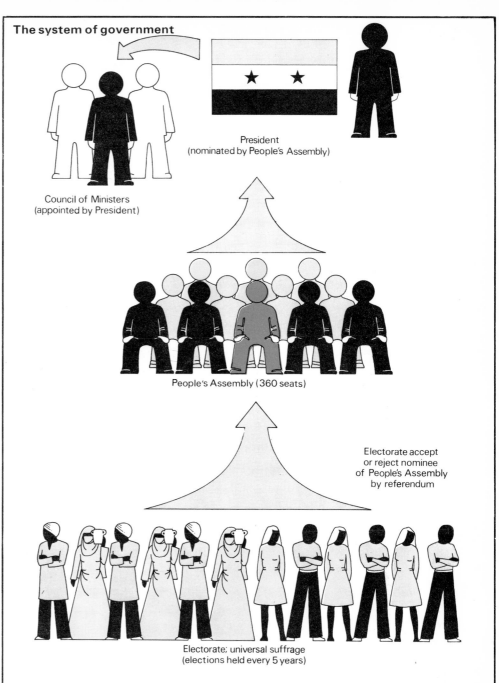

Council of Ministers
(appointed by President)

President
(nominated by People's Assembly)

People's Assembly (360 seats)

Electorate accept
or reject nominee
of People's Assembly
by referendum

Electorate; universal suffrage
(elections held every 5 years)

National Government

In theory, the structure and process of Egyptian government is straightforward. Every five years a People's Assembly is elected by universal suffrage. The Assembly nominates a President who is approved by public referendum. The President, in turn, appoints a Council of Ministers. The Assembly's formal powers are considerable. It controls the budget, can over-rule Presidential vetoes and can dismiss a Government.

In practice, however, the political process follows the injunction of Mohammed to achieve *Shura*, consultation between ruler and people, in order to arrive at *Ijma*, or consensus. The Assembly rarely divides on an issue, preferring to arrive at a common point of view, just as it prefers to avoid an open breach with the Government. This puts initiative squarely in the hands of the President.

Furthermore, there is only one political party, the Arab Socialist Union, to which all candidates for the Assembly must belong. The party, through its bi-annual congresses, determines the policies within which the Assembly legislates.

Local Government

There is a nation-wide network of elected provincial, town and village councils which use local land and building taxes, plus grants from the central government, to act on housing, health services, education, and public utilities in their areas. The majority of council members are elected, the others appointed by central government.

ANCIENT EGYPTIAN HISTORY

Prehistoric and Pre-Dynastic Periods
B.C.

To c. 3000 — Growth of the Sahara led to concentration of agricultural settlements along the Nile Valley and the Delta. Advanced irrigation methods, high degree of civilization.

Archaic Period
(from c. 3000 to 2680 B.C.)

c. 3000 — Menes unites Upper and Lower Egypt, establishes First Dynasty, rules from Memphis.

The Old Kingdom
(from c. 2680 to 2258 B.C.)

Dynasties IV to VI, contemporary with the rise of Sumer in Mesopotamia. Cheops, under whose direction the Great Pyramid at Giza was constructed, was the second pharaoh of the IV Dynasty.

The First Intermediate Period
(2258 to 2052 B.C.)

Dynasties VII-X.

The Middle Kingdom
(2150 to 1785 B.C.)

Dynasties XI and XII. The capital is transferred to Thebes. The period corresponds with the height of Minoan civilization in Crete.

The Second Intermediate Period
(1785 to 1580 B.C.)

Dynasties XII-XVII.

The New Kingdom (1580 to 1085 B.C.)

Dynasty XVIII (1580-1340 B.C.)

1515-1484 — Hatshepsut, widow of Thutmose II, rules Egypt as pharaoh.

1504-1450 — Thutmose III, after his victory at the Battle of Armageddon presides over Egyptian Empire.

1405-1370 — Amenophis III reigns over a cultural Golden Age. Builds the temple at Luxor and opposite Thebes erects the Colossi of Memnon.

1370-52 — Akhenaten abolishes polytheism, worships one god. His wife is the beautiful Nefertiti. During his rule art is more fluid and representational, less stylised.

1347-39 — Tutankhamun, pawn of the Theban priesthood, re-establishes the old cults.

Dynasty XIX (1339-1200 B.C.)

1298-32 — Ramses II re-asserts Egyptian power in Africa and Asia. He is the most commemorated of pharaohs: completion of the Hypostyle Hall at Karnak, the Ramesseum, the colossal statues at Abu Simbel.

1232-24 — Merneptah, the pharaoh of the Exodus of the Hebrews.

Dynasty XX (1200-1085 B.C.)

c. 1000 — Dorian invasions of Greece.

The Late Period (1165 to 332 B.C.)

Dynasties XXI-XXV (1085-656 B.C.)

671-663 — Fall of Memphis and Thebes to the Assyrians.

663-609 — Psammetichos I liberates Egypt from the Assyrians.

609-594 — Necho advances Egyptian forces to the banks of the Euphrates, but is defeated by Nebuchadnezzar at Carchemish. An attempt is made to dig a canal between the Mediterranean and Red Sea. Africa is circumnavigated by Phoenician seamen in Necho's service.

523 — Cambyses invades Egypt, which is now ruled by the Persian Dynasty XXVII (525-404 B.C.)

480-472 — Persian invasions, under Darius and Xerxes, of Greece are repulsed.

486-404 — Egyptian uprising against Persian rule. Dynasties XXVIII-XXX (404-341 B.C.)

343 — Persians again invade Egypt, establish their own Dynasty XXXI (341-332 B.C.). Egypt remains under foreign rule for over 2250 years.

PTOLEMAIC AND ROMAN EGYPT

332 — Alexander the Great defeats the Persians in Egypt and is welcomed as liberator. He founds Alexandria.

323 — Alexander dies and his empire is divided up amongst his generals. Ptolemy Soter acquires Egypt and extends his control over Cyrene (eastern Libya), Palestine, Cyprus, and parts of Asia Minor coast. His capital is Alexandria. The Ptolemaic Dynasty is Greek in culture and language.

323-222 — The foundations of Alexandria's cultural supremacy in the Mediterranean are laid. The Mouseion—university, research institute, artistic and literary workshop and library—is established.

c. 300 — Euclid, working in Alexandria, sets down his principles of geometry.

279 — Completion of the Pharos, the giant lighthouse in Alexandria harbour, one of the Seven Wonders of the Ancient World.

c. 230 — Eratosthenes determines that the earth is round, accurately measures its diameter.

221-51 — The dynasty declines, the power of Rome grows.

51 — Cleopatra VI becomes Queen of Egypt. Rome is engaged in civil wars. Cleopatra aims to create a Greco-Roman empire, ruled from Alexandria.

48-47 — Julius Caesar, after defeating Pompey, comes to Egypt. Cleopatra becomes his ally, follows him to Rome.

44 — Julius Caesar assassinated in Rome. The Roman world is ruled by Octavian (later Augustus) and Mark Antony. Cleopatra allies herself with Antony who bases himself in Alexandria.

31 — Civil war between Octavian and Antony. Antony, supported by the Egyptian navy, is defeated at Actium.

30 — Octavian lands in Egypt. Antony and Cleopatra commit suicide. The Ptolemaic Dynasty ends. Egypt becomes part of the Roman Empire.

A.D.

45 — St. Mark makes his first convert to Christianity in Egypt.

c. 100 — Claudius Ptolemy, geographer, works in Alexandria.

296 — Anti-Roman uprising in the Delta. The Emperor Diocletian lays siege to Alexandria, storms and loots it.

303 — Diocletian, regarding the Christians as subversives, enacts stern measures against them, which result in the martyrdom of thousands.

306-337 — Constantine, Emperor of Rome, converts to Christianity, founds Constantinople (330) and makes it capital of the Eastern Roman Empire, which includes Egypt.

324-640 — Though nominally under Eastern Roman (Byzantine) rule, Egypt rejects orthodox Christianity and is run by Coptic monks under the authority of the Coptic Patriarch of Alexandria.

451 — Council of Chalcedon brands Copts as heretics and authorizes their persecution.

ARAB AND TURKISH RULE

570 — Birth of Mohammed in Mecca.

622 — Mohammed's flight from Mecca to Medina, known as the Hegira, from which the Muslim era is reckoned.

632 — Death of Mohammed.

640 — An Arab army under the banner of Islam, led by Amr, enters Egypt.

641 — Alexandria surrenders and

660-750	welcomes Arabs as liberators from Byzantine persecution. The Ummayad Dynasty, with its capital in Damascus, rules over a united Arab Empire stretching from the borders of of China to the shores of the Atlantic, and up into France.
750	Fall of Ummayads, replaced by Abbasid Dynasty which transfers caliphate to Baghdad.
751	Arabs capture Chinese paper-makers. The use of paper spreads westwards across the Arab Empire.
756	Spain becomes independent state under Abd ar-Rahman. Over the next half century, the breakup of the Arab Empire into independent Muslim states continues.
c. 820	Copts, resentful of Arab conquerors, rise in revolt several times during the 8th and 9th centuries. After their defeat, the majority of Copts convert to Islam.
813-833	Reign of Ma'mun in Baghdad: development of Arabic letters and science.
868	Ahmed ibn Tulun, a Turkish slave, and general in the service of the Baghdad Caliphate, establishes an independent dynasty in Egypt.
910	Establishment of Fatimid Caliphate in North Africa.
969	Fatimids conquer Egypt, found Cairo.
970	Seljuk Turks enter territories of Baghdad Caliphate.
971	Al-Azhar, Cairo mosque and university, opens.
1055	Seljuks take Baghdad.
1099	Crusaders take Jerusalem.
1171	Saladin declares Fatimid Caliphate at an end, founds dynasty in Egypt and Syria.
1187	Saladin defeats Crusaders and takes Jerusalem.
1250-60	Emergence of Mameluke Sultanate in Egypt and Syria.
1453	Ottoman Turks capture Constantinople. The end of the Byzantine Empire.
1517	Ottoman Turks conquer Syria and Egypt. Ottomans rule Egypt, sometimes only nominally, until 1914.

THE MODERN PERIOD

1798-1801	French occupation of Egypt.
1805	Mohammed Ali becomes effective ruler of Egypt. First secular schools, medical school and language school established.
1851-7	Construction of Alexandria-Cairo-Suez railway.
1869	Opening of Suez Canal.
1882	Colonel Arabi Pasha's uprising against Ismail is used by Britain to justify occupation.
1883-1907	Evelyn Baring (Lord Cromer) — British Consul in Egypt and effective ruler of the country.
1902	British complete construction

	of dam at Aswan.
1918	Saad Zaghloul, nationalist leader, demands British withdrawal.
1922	British recognize Egypt as a sovereign state, but maintain army in Egypt.
1936	Anglo-Egyptian Treaty, formally ending British occupation. British army withdraws, except from Canal Zone.
1939	Completion of the Mohammed Ali Barrage at apex of the Delta, replacing barrage begun in 1843 by Ali himself.
1939-45	Egypt nominally neutral during Second World War, but British army invited to return to fight the encroaching Germans.
1948	End of British Mandate for Palestine. Establishment of state of Israel. Arab-Israeli war.

THE REVOLUTION

1918	Gamal Abdel Nasser born in Alexandria.
1948	Nasser gathers round him a group of army officers resentful of political corruption.
1952	25th January, British soldiers kill several Egyptian police in Canal Zone. 26th January, rioting in Cairo against British action and Egyptian government's inaction. 23rd July, Nasser's group stage a coup. King Farouk abdicates and leaves the country.
1953	Egypt declared a republic.
1954	General Neguib forced into retirement. Nasser becomes head of state.
1954-56	British evacuate the Canal Zone.
1956	United States cancels loan to Egypt for construction of High Dam at Aswan. Nasser nationalizes Suez Canal to use revenues to pay for High Dam. Israel invades Sinai. Britain and France land troops in Canal Zone. Britain and France withdraw after international protest.
1958-61	Egypt and Syria combine to form the short-lived United Arab Republic (name retained until 1971).
1961	Nasser introduces sweeping socialist measures, limiting incomes, nationalizing banks and cotton industry, further redistributing land.
1967	The June "Six Day War". Israel attacks and defeats Egypt, occupies all of Sinai. Suez Canal is blocked.
1970	September, Nasser dies. Anwar Sadat becomes President.
1971	Egypt's official name becomes the Arab Republic of Egypt (A.R.E.).
1973	October, Egyptian forces cross the Canal and drive back the Israeli army. Israeli forces continue to occupy Gaza Strip

1975	and most of Sinai. June, Suez Canal re-opened.

PHARAONIC GODS

Supreme among the gods was Ra, the god of the Sun, also called Amen-Ra. Osiris, his son, ruled on earth until he was murdered by Set, his brother, god of Darkness. The wife of Osiris was Isis, goddess of Heaven and Earth. Their child, Horus, became Lord of Earth, and Osiris, the god of the Underworld, Judge of the Dead.

The gods originated in the times before Egypt was united, and was instead organized into local and regional units. Therefore, the gods of one locality might have had many of the qualities of gods from other parts of the country. Each god usually combined human with animal attributes, such as speed, keen sight or strength, and so each god is usually represented by a particular animal which itself was considered sacred by the followers of that cult.

Amen-Ra, the sun-god, patron deity of Thebes. Associated with the ram and hawk.

Anubis, god of the dead, patron deity in certain parts of Upper Egypt. Associated with the jackal.

Atoum, god of the setting sun, associated with the lion and snake.

Hathor, goddess of heaven, joy and love. Deity of Denderah and protector of the Theban necropolis. Associated with the cow.

Horus, represented by the winged sun disc, and associated with the falcon.

Isis, goddess of heaven and earth, patron goddess of Philae, wife of Osiris and mother of Horus. Associated with the vulture.

Khnum, patron god of Elephantine Island and the Cataracts. Associated with the ram.

Maat, goddess of justice. Associated with the ostrich feather.

Osiris, god of the underworld.

Ptah, patron god of Memphis and father of the gods. Identified with the bull.

Sobek, god of the waters, patron of Faiyum, associated with the crocodile.

Thoth, god of science and patron god of Hermopolis, associated with the ibis.

Reference
The Economy

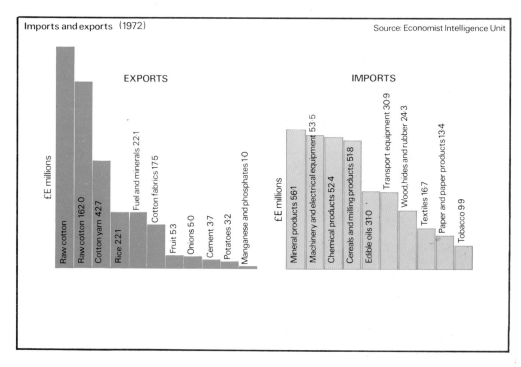

FACTS AND FIGURES

Total wealth produced: (GNP 1974 estimate) £E3,636 million.
GNP per head: £E101.
Economic growth: (1973) 3.9%.
Main sources of income:
Agriculture: cotton, rice, sugar cane, maize, corn, sorghum, barley, onions, watermelons, dates and citrus fruits.
Mining: oil, natural gas, manganese, phosphates and iron. Hydro-electric power from the Aswan High Dam is being exploited and oil resources are being developed.
Industry: textiles, food processing, cement, fertilizers, steel, small-scale machinery, handicrafts. Tourism, and the recently re-opened Suez Canal, are expected to make growing contributions.
Main trading partners: USSR, Australia, France, USA, Britain, West Germany, Italy, Czechoslovakia, India, Brazil.
Currency: £E1 = 100 piastres = 1,000 milliemes.
£1 = £E0.93 (1975) — official rate.
£1 = £E1.450 (1975) — incentive or tourist rate.

The Economy

The October 1973 war had less effect on the country's economy than was at first thought, but it weakened Egypt's financial position. Debts, principally to communist countries, increased enormously though Arab states are now investing in Egypt.

The need for Egypt to earn foreign money is greater than ever. This will partly be achieved by encouraging tourism and by collecting Suez Canal fees. But the brunt of the task falls to increasing exports, while attempting to cut down on imports. The strategy is to develop Egypt away from basic dependence on agriculture and build industry into the largest sector.

The industrial sector is increasing output at the rate of nearly 10% per annum. The Helwan Steel Works began production in 1958. An oil pipeline is being constructed between Suez and the Mediterranean, with a refinery being built in Alexandria. However, the older industries of textiles and food processing still account for the major share of industrial earnings.

Imports and exports (1972) Source: Economist Intelligence Unit

EXPORTS

£E millions
Raw cotton
Raw cotton 162.0
Cotton yarn 427
Rice 221
Fuel and minerals 221
Cotton fabrics 175
Fruit 53
Onions 50
Cement 37
Potatoes 32
Manganese and phosphates 10

IMPORTS

£E millions
Mineral products 561
Machinery and electrical equipment 53.5
Chemical products 52.4
Cereals and milling products 518
Edible oils 31.0
Transport equipment 30.9
Wood, hides and rubber 24.3
Textiles 16.7
Paper and paper products 13.4
Tobacco 9.9

Sugar Cane   Rice   Industrial Fishing

Oases

Cotton   Sponge Fishing   Principal Food Crops

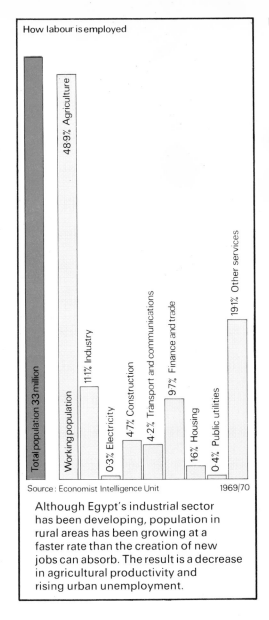

How labour is employed

Total population 33 million

Working population

48.9% Agriculture

11.1% Industry

0.3% Electricity

4.7% Construction

4.2% Transport and communications

9.7% Finance and trade

1.6% Housing

0.4% Public utilities

19.1% Other services

Source: Economist Intelligence Unit

1969/70

Although Egypt's industrial sector has been developing, population in rural areas has been growing at a faster rate than the creation of new jobs can absorb. The result is a decrease in agricultural productivity and rising urban unemployment.

Industry in Egypt

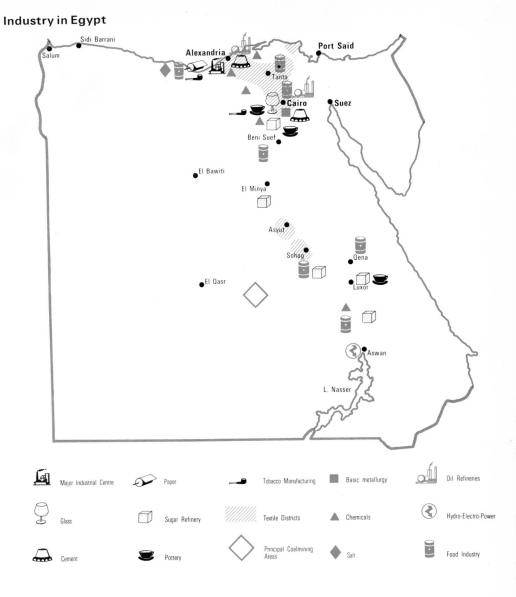

Major Industrial Centre	Paper	Tobacco Manufacturing	Basic metallurgy
Glass	Sugar Refinery	Textile Districts	Chemicals
Cement	Pottery	Principal Coalmining Areas	Salt
			Oil Refineries
			Hydro-Electro-Power
			Food Industry

The problems of growth

Apart from the strains that war has put on the Egyptian economy, the country's real battle is in trying to feed her fast-expanding population, now increasing at the rate of 2.5% a year.

The chart indicates the problem. Egypt's industrial sector has been growing much faster than her agricultural sector. In so far as consumption of cotton textiles reflects personal benefits deriving from this growth, the situation has steadily improved. However, in terms of the consumption of calories and proteins, the gains made in the Fifties and early Sixties have recently been eroded by population growth. Egypt is losing the battle for food.

Population growth has caused setbacks in other areas too, such as the quality of urban life which has suffered, particularly due to the failure of the public transport system to match capacity to demand. On the other hand, Egyptians have benefited from better services such as education, health and social services.

Per capita consumption of food and textiles   Source: Central Agency for Public Mobilisation and Statistics (Cairo)

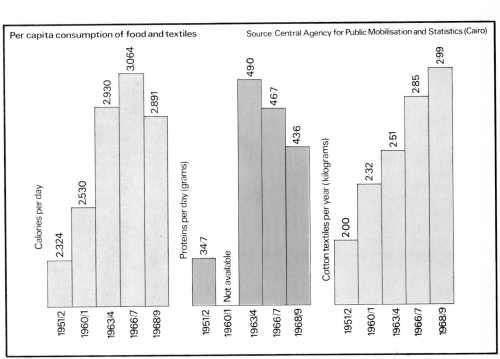

Calories per day: 2,324 (1951/2), 2,530 (1960/1), 2,930 (1963/4), 3,064 (1966/7), 2,891 (1968/9)

Proteins per day (grams): 34.7 (1951/2), Not available (1960/1), 490 (1963/4), 467 (1966/7), 436 (1968/9)

Cotton textiles per year (kilograms): 2.00 (1951/2), 2.32 (1960/1), 2.51 (1963/4), 2.85 (1966/7), 2.99 (1968/9)

Gazetteer

Abu Simbel (22 24N 31 29E) Site on left bank of Nile 233 km. (145 miles) S.W. of Aswan, with two temples of Ramses II (1304-1237 B.C.) in sandstone cliffs. Temples removed and re-sited 61 m. (200 ft.) above original site 1964-8.

Alamein, El (30 40N 20 0E) Village on Mediterranean coastal railway 103 km. (65 miles) S.W. of Alexandria. Germans defeated there by British in 1942.

Alexandria (31 5N 29 45E) **El Iskandariya.** Pop. (1971) 2,086,000. Chief seaport, between the Mediterranean and Lake Mareotis. Exports raw cotton. Cotton ginning. Cottonseed oil pressing. Manufactures paper and soap. Airports. Many resident foreign traders, mostly Greek and Syrian. Founded in 332 B.C. by Alexander of Macedonia; became centre of Hellenistic and Jewish culture. Later a Christian centre. Taken by Arabs in 7th century. Linked to the Nile during 19th century by Mahmudiya Canal, and became commercially important. Ancient granite shaft called Pompey's Pillar. Catacombs. Ancient ruins at Pharos.

Aswan (24 12N 32 59E) Ancient Syrene. Pop. (1971) 682,000. Town on the Nile below the first cataract. Commercial centre and tourist centre. Winter resort. Granite quarries. Railway to Cairo. Aswan Irrigation Dam 5 km. (3 miles) upstream, completed in 1902. Aswan High Dam, 1960-70.

Asyût (27 15N 31 0E) Ancient Lycopolis. Pop. (1971) 1,502,000. Coptic centre. Caravan trading. Pottery. Cotton spinning. Wood and ivory carving.

Cairo (30 1N 31 14E) **El Qahira.** Pop. (1971) 5,139,000. Capital of Egypt and largest city in Africa. On the Delta. Chief commercial centre and international airport. Manufactures cement, textiles, vegetable oils, beer, paper. Printing industry. Old Cairo was founded in 641 A.D. by Arabs, as El Fustat. Al Qahira founded in 968; attacked by Crusaders and successfully defended in 1176; in same year Saladin's Citadel was built on Moqattam Hills. Turkish 1517-1798. Rapid physical and commercial growth during 19th century and into 20th. Mosque and University of Al Azhar founded 971. Chief Seminary of Islamic Theology. Cairo University 1908. Ein Shams University 1950. Over 200 mosques and many Coptic churches. Many museums, including Museum of Antiquities. Opera house and government offices, in European style in West Cairo.

Eastern Desert (28 0N 32 30E) Rocky area between the E. bank of the Nile and the Red Sea. Mountainous along the coast. Highest peak is Shayib el Banat, 2,195 m. (7,175 ft.)

Faiyum, El (29 20N 30 59E) Pop. (1971) 1,204,000. Capital of El Faiyum governorate 88 km. (55 miles) S.W. of Cairo, in El Faiyum Oasis. Road and railway to Nile Valley. Cotton ginning, spinning, weaving wool and cotton. Dyeing. Tanning. Old city of Crocodilopolis, also called Arsinoe, excavated to north of it.

Giza (30 0N 31 0E) **El Gizeh.** Pop. (1971) 1,999,000. Capital of Giza governorate, on west bank of Nile opposite Cairo. Manufactures textiles and footwear. 8 km. (5 miles) to S.W. are the Great Pyramid of Khufu (Cheops) which covers 5 hectares (13 acres) and the Sphinx, and pyramids of Khafra and Menkaura.

Karnak (25 40N 32 38E) Village on site of north part of Thebes. Ruins of temples.

Kharga Oasis (25 30N 30 33E) Largest and most southerly Egyptian oasis, in a low area of the Western Desert. 161 km. (100 miles) long N-S; greatest width E-W 80 km. (50 miles). The population is mostly Berber. Dates and cereals grown. Chief town is El Kharga. Railway to the Nile.

Luxor (25 40N 32 38E) Pop. c.30,000. Winter resort on site of ancient Thebes. Archaeological discoveries in ruins of old city; best known is tomb of Tutankhamun, excavated in 1922.

Mahalla el Kubra (31 10N 31 0E) Town on the Delta. Pop. (1966) 225,000. Centre of textile industry. Cotton, rice, cereals grown in surrounding region.

Mansura (31 0N 31 20E) Town on Damietta branch of the Nile. Pop. (1966) 191,000. Capital of Daqahliya governorate. Railway junction. Manufactures cotton. In 1250 the Mamelukes defeated St. Louis here.

Mareotis, Lake (31 0N 30 0E) **Mariut.** Salt lake in the Delta, divided from the Mediterranean by narrow strip of land on which Alexandria is built.

Mediterranean Sea (36 0N 15 0E) Ancient *Mare Internum.* Area 2,520,000 sq. km. (970,000 sq. miles), excluding the Black Sea. W-E 3,700 km. (2,300 miles) long. Fairly high salinity. Almost tideless. Joined in S.E. to the Red Sea, by the Suez Canal and Gulf of Suez. Commercially important from ancient times up to late 15th century; declined after Cape route to India was discovered; revived when Suez Canal was opened in 1869.

Minya, El (28 12N 30 30E) Pop. (1971) 1,837,000. Capital of Minya governorate, on left bank of Nile 217 km. (135 miles) S. of Cairo. River port. Trade in cotton and cereals. Sugar refining, cotton ginning.

Nasser, Lake (24 0N 32 40E) Large artificial lake made by the Aswan High Dam. Silts easily.

Nile, River (27 20N 31 0E) White Nile is longest river in Africa: 5,608 km. (3,485 miles) from Lake Victoria, its source. Enters Egypt after winding through the Sudd and receiving the Blue Nile at Khartoum in Sudan. White Nile and Blue Nile then flow to Mediterranean as one river. Before Aswan the river flows through a narrow valley, with 6 cataracts; after Aswan, the valley widens. River divides at the Delta into the Rosetta Channel in W. and the Damietta in E. The Blue Nile rises in the Ethiopian Highlands and receives heavy monsoon rains in summer. The Nile used to overflow its Egyptian banks every year, from late August to early September. This made agriculture possible. At high water, the Nile was navigable throughout its whole length in Egypt; at low water, it was not navigable below Aswan.

Port Said (31 28N 32 6E) Pop. (1971) 320,000. Seaport on the Mediterranean, at entrance to Suez Canal, 161 km. (100 miles) N.E. of Cairo, between Lake Manzala and the Mediterranean. Fuelling station. Exports cotton. Manufactures chemicals and cigarettes. Salt panning. Founded in 1859, and named after Khedive Said.

Qattara Depression (30 0N 28 0E) Low area, with a salt marsh, in the Western Desert. 289 km. (180 miles) long N.E.-S.W.; greatest width 120 km. 75 miles). Lowest part is 133 m. (436 ft.) below sea level.

Red Sea (20 0N 39 0E) Sea between N.E. Africa and S.W. Asia. 2,414 km. (1,500 miles) long from Suez to Bab el Mandeb (Strait of Tears). Greatest width 337 km. (210 miles). N. part divided by Sinai Peninsula, into W. Gulf of Suez and E. Gulf of Aqaba. Suez Canal to the Mediterranean. Receives few rivers. Low rainfall; high salinity. Chief Egyptian port is Suez.

Sinai Peninsula (28 40N 33 40E) Pop. (1960) 50,000. Between Gulf of Suez in W. and Gulf of Aqaba in E. Sand dunes along Mediterranean coast. Centre mountainous plateau El Tih: highest peak Jebel Katrin, 2,637 m. (8,652 ft.). Barren, very little water. Occupied by Israeli army in 1967.

Suez (30 0N 32 30E) Pop. (1971) 327,000. Oil-fuelling station. Oil refining. Manufactures fertilizers. Much damage during June 1967 Arab-Israeli war and Israeli bombardment up to 1970.

Suez Canal (30 30N 32 15E). 165 km. (103 miles) long. Connects Mediterranean and Red Sea. Designed by French engineer F. de Lesseps; opened in 1869. Narrowest width 60 m. (197 ft.) Takes ships of 11 m. (37 ft.) Draught. Convention of Constantinople (1888) opened it to all nations. Owned by the Suez Canal Co. 1875-1956. Nationalized in 1956. Closed in June 1967, because of Arab-Israeli conflict. Re-opened June 1975.

Suez, Gulf of (29 0N 33 0E) N.W. arm of Red Sea: 273 km. (170 miles) long; widest point 40 km. (25 miles). Contains Egypt's major oilfields.

Tanta (30 50N 30 48E) Town on Delta. Pop. (1966) 230,000. Capital of Gharbiya governorate. Railway junction. Commercial centre. Manufactures soap. Cotton ginning; Pressing of cottonseed oil. Famous for fairs and feasts.

Western Desert (27 0N 27 0E) Part of Libyan Desert, W. of Nile. Sandy, hardly any rain.

Zagazig (30 33N 31 12E) Town on Delta. Pop. (1966) 151,000. Capital of Sharqiya governorate. Canal and railway junction. Cotton mills. Trade in cotton and grain. In a fertile region. Ruins of Bubastis to S.

Index

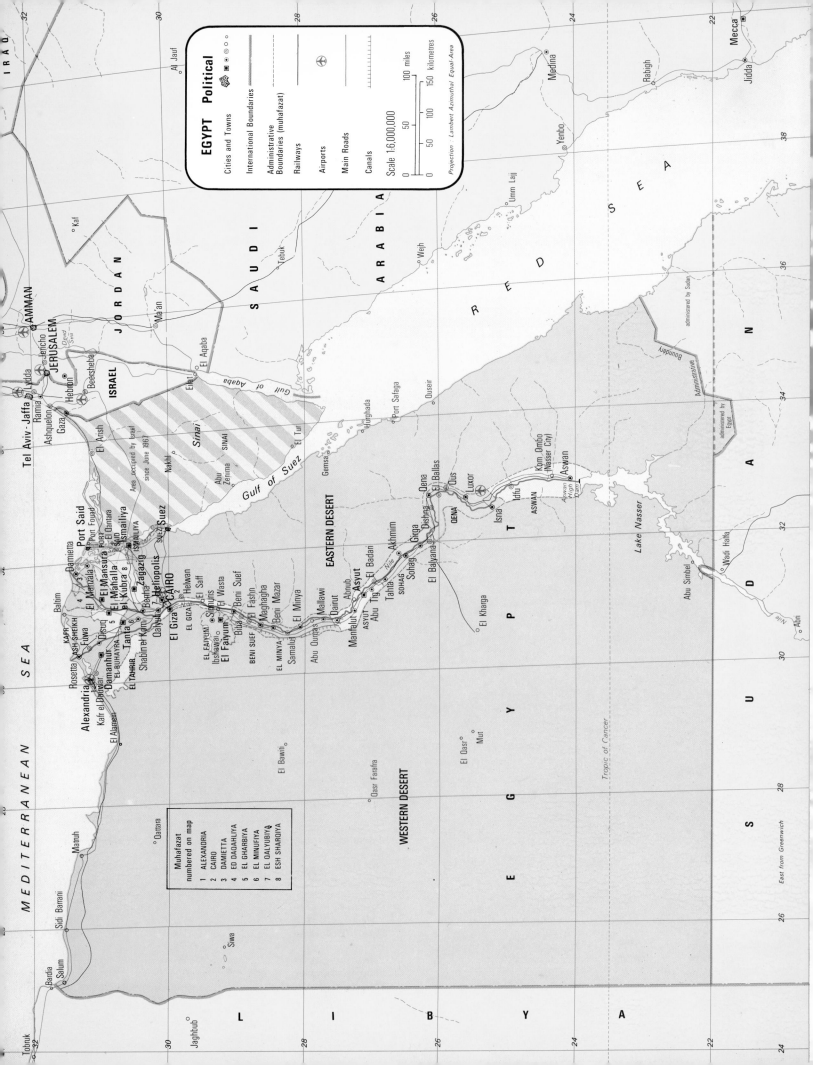

EGYPT Political

Cities and Towns

International Boundaries

Administrative
Boundaries (muhafazat)

Railways

Airports

Main Roads

Canals

Scale 1:6,000,000

100 miles

150 kilometres

Projection - Lambert Azimuthal Equal-Area

Muhafazat
numbered on map
1 ALEXANDRIA
2 CAIRO
3 ED DAQAHLIYA
4 EL GHARBIYA
5 EL MINUFIYA
6 EL QALYUBIYA
7 ESH SHARQIYA

IRAQ

Al Jauf

SAUDI ARABIA

Kaf

Ma'an

JORDAN

AMMAN

Jericho
JERUSALEM
Lydda
Ramla
Hebron
Beersheba
Tel Aviv - Jaffa
Ashquelon
Gaza
ISRAEL

El Arish

Nakhl

Abu Zenima

Sinai
SINAI

El Tur

Area occupied by Israel
since June 1967

Port Said
Port Fouad
El Qantara
Ismailiya
ISMAILIYA
Suez
Suez

Gulf of Suez

Gulf of Aqaba

Eilat
El Aqaba

Tebuk

Wejh

Umm Lajj

Medina

Rabigh

Jidda

Mecca

Yenbo

RED SEA

MEDITERRANEAN SEA

Damietta
Rosetta
Baltim
KAFR ASH-SHEIKH
Alexandria
Kafr el Dawar
Damanhur
EL-BUHAYRA
El Alamein
Matruh
Sidi Barrani
Salum
Bardia
Tobruk

Fuwa
Disuq
EL TAHRIR
Shabin el Kom
Tanta
Benha
Damietta
El Mansura
El Mahalla
El Kubra
Zagazig
Qalyub
Heliopolis
CAIRO
El Giza
EL GIZA
Helwan
El Saff
El Wasta

Port Said

El Menzala

Jaghbub

Qattara

Siwa

El Qasr
Mut

Qasr Farafra

El Bawiti

WESTERN DESERT

El Kharga

EASTERN DESERT

Beni Suef
BENI SUEF
El Faiyum
EL FAIYUM
Ibshaway
El Fayum
Biba
El Fashn
Maghagha
Beni Mazar
Samalut
El Minya
EL MINYA
Abu Qurqas
Mallawi
Dairut
Manfalut
Abnub
Asyut
ASYUT
Abu Tig
El Badari
Tahta
Akhmim
SOHAG
Sohag
Gitga
Dishna
El Balyana
QENA
Qena
El Ballas
Qus
Luxor
Isna
Idfu
ASWAN
Kom Ombo
(Nasser City)
Aswan
Aswan High Dam

Gemsa

Hurghada

Port Safaga

Quseir

Lake Nasser

Abu Simbel

Wadi Halfa

Abri

SUDAN

administered by Sudan

administered by Egypt

Administrative Boundary

Tropic of Cancer

LIBYA

EGYPT

East from Greenwich

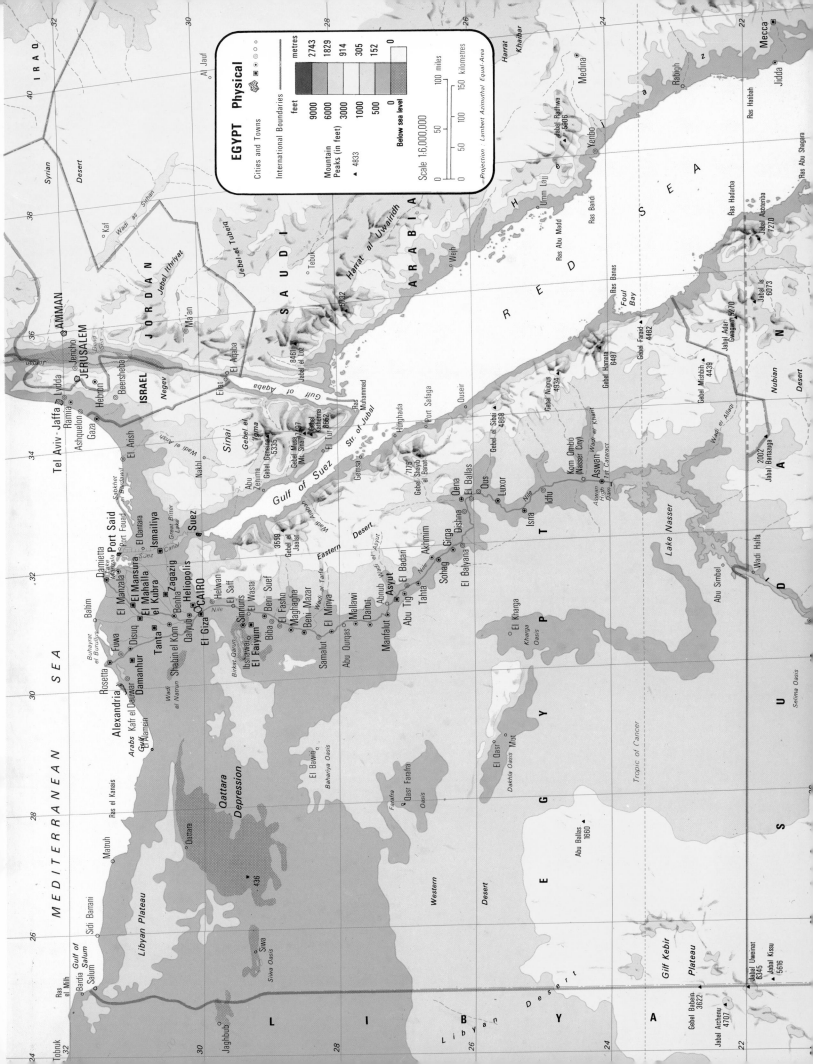

EGYPT Physical

Cities and Towns

International Boundaries

	metres	feet
	2743	9000
	1829	6000
	914	3000
	305	1000
	152	500
	0	0

Mountain Peaks (in feet) ▲ 4833

Below sea level

Scale 1:6,000,000

100 miles
150 kilometres
50   100
0   50   100

Projection : Lambert Azimuthal Equal-Area

I R A Q

Al Jauf

Syrian

Desert

Wadi as Sirhan

o Kaf

Jebel et Tubeiq

Jebel Ithriyat

AMMAN
JERUSALEM
o Jericho
Lydda
Ramla
ISRAEL
Tel Aviv-Jaffa
Ashquelon
Gaza
Hebron
Beersheba
Negev

Dead Sea

Jordan

J O R D A N

Ma'an

El Arish

El Qantara

El Arish

Wadi el Arish

Nakhl

Sinai

Sabkhet el Bardawil

S A U D I

Tebuk

Jebel el Loz 8461

Jabal el Loz

El Aqaba

Elat

Gulf of Aqaba

Gebel el Igma

Gebel Geneisa 5335

Abu Zenima

Gebel Musa (Mt. Sinai) 7497

Gebel Katherina 8662

El Tur

6732

Harrat al Uwairidh

Wejh

Ras Abu Madd

Umm Lajj

A R A B I A

Medina

Rabigh

Mecca

Jidda

Ras Hatiba

Jabal Radhwa 5806

Yenbo

Ras Baridi

R E D

S E A

Foul Bay

Ras Banas

Ras Hadarba

Jabal Astoriba 7270

Jabal Is 6073

Ras Abu Shagara

N

U

B

I

A

N

Nubian

Desert

M E D I T E R R A N E A N   S E A

Tobruk

Ras el Milh

Bardia

Salum

Gulf of Salum

Sidi Barrani

Ras el Kanais

Matruh

Libyan Plateau

Qattara

Qattara Depression

436

Siwa
Siwa Oasis

Jaghbub

L   I   B

Damietta
Port Said
Port Fouad
El Manzala
Lake Manzala
Rosetta
Baltim
Fuwa
Disuq
Kafr el Dauwar
Damanhur
Alexandria
Arabs
El Alamein
Buhayrat el Burullus

Ismailiya
Suez
Suez Canal
Great Bitter Lake
Port Said

El Mansura
El Manzala
El Mahalla el Kubra
Tanta
Shabin el Kom
Qalyub
Benha
Zagazig
Heliopolis
CAIRO
El Giza
Birkat Qarun
Ibshawai
El Faiyum
Biba
Wadi el Natrun

Helwan
El Saff
El Wasta
Beni Suef
Maghagha
Beni-Mazar
El Minya
Mallawi
Dairut
Abu Qurqas
Samalut
Manfalut
Asyut
El Badari
Abu Tig
Tahta
Akhmim
Sohag
Girga
El Balyana
Dishna
Qena
El Ballas
Qus
Luxor
Isna
Idfu
Kom Ombo (Nasser Cnl)
Aswan
Aswan High Dam
1st Cataract

El Bawiti
Bahariya Oasis

Qasr Farafra
Farafra Oasis
Faafra

El Kharga
Kharga Oasis

El Qasr
Mut
Dakhla Oasis

Tropic of Cancer

Western

Desert

E   G   Y   P   T

Abu Ballas 1660

Gilf Kebir Plateau

Gebel Babein 3622

Jabal Archenu 4707

Jabal Uweinat 6345

Jabal Kissu 5616

Y

A

Libyan Desert

Nile

Wadi el Tarfa

Eastern

Desert

Wadi el Asyut

Wadi el Kharit

Wadi el Allaqi

Lake Nasser

Wadi Halfa

Abu Simbel

Selima Oasis

Hurghada

Port Safaga

Quseir

Gemsa

Str. of Jubal

Gebel Shayib el Banat 7175

Ras Muhammad

Gulf of Suez

Gebel el Jaalal 3559

Wadi Araba

Gebel Sibai 4868

Gebel Nugus 4934

Gebel Hamata 6487

Gebel Faraid 4482

Jabal Adar Qwagwan 5270

Gebel Mishbih 4439

2002

Jabal Bartazuga